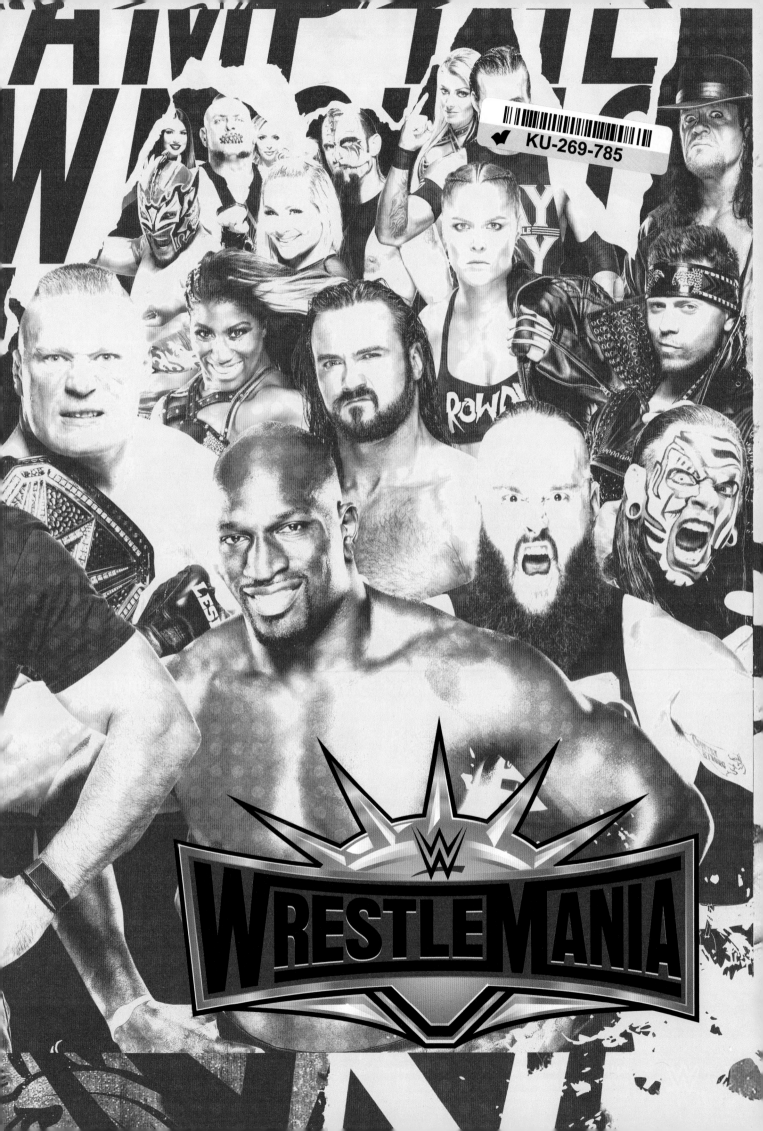

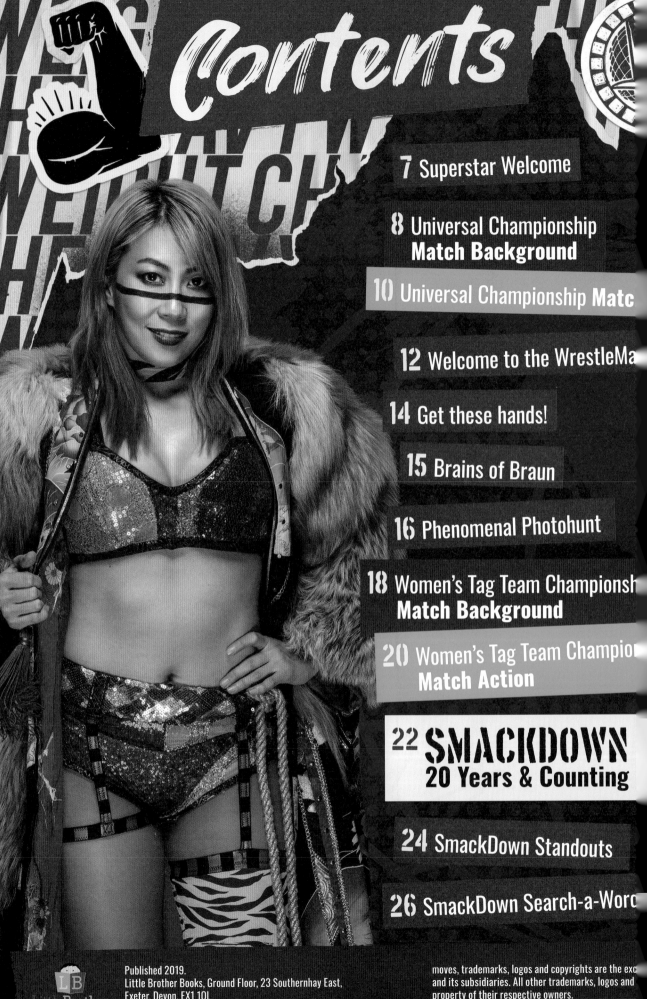

Contents

Published 2019.
Little Brother Books, Ground Floor, 23 Southernhay East,
Exeter, Devon, EX1 1QL
Printed In Poland.
books@littlebrotherbooks.co.uk | www.littlebrotherbooks.co.uk
The Little Brother Books trademark, email and website addresses, are the
sole and exclusive properties of Little Brother Books Limited.
All W programming, talent names, images, likenesses, slogans, wrestling

HANDS OFF!

THIS BELONGS TO...

Cameron!!

HEY THERE!

WWE UNIVERSE... *SETH FREAKING ROLLINS* HERE! BESIDES BURNING IT DOWN IN THE WWE RING, NOTHING *THRILLS ME MORE* THAN TO PRESENT THE *2020 WWE ANNUAL!*

INSIDE THESE *ACTION-PACKED PAGES,* YOU'LL HAVE A CHANCE TO *SLAY* ALL SORTS OF ACTIVITIES- FROM QUIZ GAMES TO CROSSWORDS, PHOTO HUNTS, MAZES AND MUCH MORE! YOU'LL EVEN *WRITE A SONG WITH ELIAS,* EXPLORE THE MIND OF BRAUN STROWMAN (YIKES!), AND CELEBRATE *20 YEARS OF SMACKDOWN!*

OF COURSE, YOU'LL ALSO RELIVE ALL THE *EXPLOSIVE ACTION* FROM *WRESTLEMANIA 35,* STARTING WITH MY FAVOURITE MATCH OF THE NIGHT. *TURN THE PAGE!*

DING! DING!

UNIVERSAL CHAMPIONSHIP MATCH

BACKGROUND

THE COMPETITORS

By now, you've grown weary of Lesnar's advocate, Paul Heyman, singing his praises. Is he annoying? Yes. Infuriating? For sure. But wrong? Here are the facts. Lesnar is the Beast who once **decimated John Cena** with sixteen German Suplexes, **pummeled Randy Orton** to a pulp and **battered Roman Reigns** in the main event of *WrestleMania*. If that is not enough, he also did what 21 men straight could not defeat Undertaker on the Grandest Stage. You may not see him very often, but when you do, chaos and destruction follow.

BROCK LESNAR
(WITH PAUL HEYMAN)

THE BUILD-UP....

Like a real life action hero, Seth Rollins competes as if the fate of the WWE Universe rests squarely on his shoulders. Since The Shield went their separate ways, Seth has been "**burning it down**" on his own, leaving every ounce of sweat and energy on the mat. With the muscle to match up with the big boys and the agility to move like a cruiserweight, **Rollins is ready for any challenge.** This sports entertainment prototype is just getting started and appears primed to lead WWE into the future.

VS SETH ROLLINS

The reign of Universal Champion Brock Lesnar was rarely in doubt for the better part of a year. Enter Rollins, the 2019 Royal Rumble winner and a Superstar known for toppling dynasties. Facing a choice of who to challenge at *WrestleMania*, chants of "**Slay the Beast**" were all the motivation Rollins needed to choose Lesnar. **The WWE Universe longed for a new champion.** To give them one, Seth needed to do what both his former Shield-mates tried and failed to do, take down Lesnar one-on-one at *WrestleMania*.

WRESTLEMANIA UNIVERSAL CHAMPIONSHIP MATCH

ACTION BROCK LESNAR VS SETH ROLLINS

(WITH PAUL HEYMAN)

WHAT A *WRESTLEMANIA* INTRODUCTION BY ALEXA BLISS! WAIT? WHAT THE HECK IS PAUL HEYMAN DOING HERE?

HEYMAN HAS DEMANDED THE UNIVERSAL CHAMPIONSHIP MATCH START RIGHT NOW! AND NOW LESNAR ATTACKS ROLLINS BEFORE THE BELL!

THE MATCH HASN'T EVEN STARTED AND SETH IS TAKING A BEATING.

F5 TO THE FLOOR!

LESNAR ORDERS THE REF TO RING THE BELL. BUT IS ROLLINS OK?

THE REIGNING CHAMP HURLS HIM INTO THE SIDE OF THE RING...

WELCOME TO THE WRESTLEMANIA BIG QUIZ

Another year, another hard-hitting WWE Annual full of fun facts and rousing *WrestleMania* action! I'm John Cena, and I'm here to make sure you have what it takes for WWE's grandest stage. Want to impress a 16-time Champ? Flex your mental muscle on 16 'Mania-themed brain-busters!

WRESTLEMANIA RECORDS

1 Who broke the *WrestleMania* record for fastest victory by pinning Erick Rowan in 6 seconds?

- Ⓐ Triple H ☐
- Ⓑ The Rock ☑
- Ⓒ Stone Cold Steve Austin ☐
- Ⓓ Undertaker ☐

2 Undertaker won a record 21 straight *WrestleMania* matches. Who broke his winning streak?

- Ⓐ John Cena ☐
- Ⓑ Roman Reigns ☐
- Ⓒ Shawn Michaels ☐
- Ⓓ Brock Lesnar ☑

3 What legendary ring announcer appeared at the first 32 *WrestleManias*?

- Ⓐ Howard Finkel ☐
- Ⓑ Lilian Garcia ☐
- Ⓒ Tony Chimel ☑
- Ⓓ None of the above ☐

4 Who is the only Superstar to win four matches in one *WrestleMania*?

- Ⓐ Daniel Bryan ☐
- Ⓑ Yokozuna ☐
- Ⓒ "Macho Man" Randy Savage ☑
- Ⓓ Bret Hart ☐

5 Who won the fastest match in *WrestleMania* history with a World Title on the line?

- Ⓐ Rey Mysterio ☐
- Ⓑ Sheamus ☑
- Ⓒ Hulk Hogan ☐
- Ⓓ Kane ☐

6 How many times did the Hardcore Championship change hands at *WrestleMania X8*?

- Ⓐ 2 ✓
- Ⓑ 3
- Ⓒ 4
- Ⓓ 5

7 Who hit Jeff Hardy with a Spear from atop a ladder at *WrestleMania X-7*?

- Ⓐ Matt Hardy
- Ⓑ Edge ✓
- Ⓒ Christian
- Ⓓ Spike Dudley

8 Who did boxer Mike Tyson punch out at *WrestleMania 14*?

- Ⓐ Shawn Michaels
- Ⓑ Triple H
- Ⓒ Stone Cold Steve Austin
- Ⓓ Mr. McMahon ✓

9 Who leapt from the top of the Hell in a Cell stage and crashed through a table at *WrestleMania 32*?

- Ⓐ Shane McMahon ✓
- Ⓑ Edge
- Ⓒ Mick Foley
- Ⓓ Jeff Hardy

10 Who got revenge on Mr. McMahon at *WrestleMania X-7* by smacking him in the face?

- Ⓐ Lita
- Ⓑ Jacqueline
- Ⓒ Trish Stratus •
- Ⓓ Chyna ✓

THE ROAD TO WRESTLEMANIA 35

11 Who was not in the Gauntlet Match that Kofi Kingston won to prove himself worthy of a WWE Title opportunity?

- Ⓐ Sheamus ✓
- Ⓒ Kevin Owens
- Ⓑ Samoa Joe
- Ⓓ Rowan

12 Which champion laid the championship down at Stephanie McMahon's feet demanding Becky Lynch be given a title opportunity?

- Ⓐ Ronda Rousey
- Ⓒ Sasha Banks
- Ⓑ Asuka
- Ⓓ Bayley ✓

13 What type of match did the Boss & Hug Connection win to become the first WWE Women's Tag Team Champions?

- Ⓐ Ladder Match
- Ⓒ Tables Match
- Ⓑ Elimination Chamber
- Ⓓ Falls Count Anywhere ✓

14 Who did Batista attack to provoke Triple H into a *WrestleMania* clash?

- Ⓐ Undertaker
- Ⓒ Randy Orton
- Ⓑ Ric Flair ✓
- Ⓓ Mr. McMahon

15 To earn an Intercontinental Championship Match, Finn Balor won a Handicap Match against Bobby Lashley and who?

- Ⓐ Lio Rush ✓
- Ⓒ Dolph Ziggler
- Ⓑ Drew McIntyre
- Ⓓ Jinder Mahal

16

What three Superstars have faced John Cena twice at *WrestleMania*?

RESPECT

Answers on pages 76-77

GET THESE HANDS!

When I find these WWE Superstars, they are going to get these hands! The trouble is... I can only *see* their hands! Help me figure out which bodies they belong to, or there is no telling what I might destroy next!

1 AJ

2 Finn balor

3 rey mysterio

4 Alexsa bliss

5 brock lesnar

6 samoa

7 ronda rousey

Answers on pages 76-77

14

Brains of BRAUN

A Monster Among Men has a lot on his mind, from vehicles in need of dismantling to the unfortunate souls he is not finished with! You might not be Nicolas, but you can help him win the gold by finishing his thoughts!

1 IS MR MCMAHON STILL UPSET THAT I FLIPPED HIS _limousine_ IN JANUARY 2019?

2 I STILL HAVE THE BEST BEARD OF THE _Wyatt_ FAMILY, MY FORMER TEAM.

3 I MISS MY "TEAM LITTLE BIG" PARTNER _Alexa bliss_ FROM THE MIXED MATCH CHALLENGE.

4 DID NICOLAS REALLY GIVE UP THE TAG TEAM TITLES TO ATTEND _4th grade_

5 I NEED A BIGGER TROPHY SHELF AFTER WINNING THE 2018 _greatest_ ROYAL RUMBLE.

LIMOUSINE
WYATT
4TH GRADE
ALEXA BLISS
GREATEST

Answers on pages 76-77

PHENOMENAL PHOTOHUNT

When you walk around calling yourself "phenomenal," you had better back it up in the ring! That is why I live to dazzle the WWE Universe with moves like these. Of course, some sneaky editor (or perhaps Daniel Bryan) has made all sorts of crafty changes! Use your eagle eye to help me spot eight differences between each picture.

WOMEN'S TAG TEAM CHAMPIONSHIP MATCH

BACKGROUND

THE COMPETITORS

SASHA BANKS & BAYLEY

Aptly named The Boss & Hug Connection, Sasha and Bayley share a fascinating history. At odds for much of their careers, their bitter rivalry **blossomed into a close friendship**. After a series of spats, they entered friendship therapy to patch things up! Once they did, they became **unstoppable** and helped **inspire** WWE's new Women's Tag Team Division.

THE IICONICS

Aussie Superstars Billie Kay and Peyton Royce sure think highly of themselves. Their **haughty attitude** is rough on the ears but there is no denying their talent. This outspoken pair is determined to live up to their name and become **true icons** in WWE.

THE BUILD-UP...

FATAL 4-WAY MATCH
FOR THE WWE WOMEN'S TAG TEAM CHAMPIONSHIP

NIA JAX & TAMINA

Both of these **powerful women** are imposing enough alone. Standing side by side, they are downright scary. Nia overpowered Alexa Bliss at *WrestleMania 34* to win the Raw Women's Championship, while Tamina has been pushing fellow Superstars around for a decade. If they can find **the right chemistry** in the ring, look out!

BETH PHOENIX & NATALYA

A decade ago, these friends were ahead of their time. Known as **"The Divas of Doom,"** Beth and Nattie won the first-ever Divas Tag Team Tables Match. Now reunited, these **revolutionary Superstars** hope experience gives them the edge over their competition. As the Women's Evolution comes full circle, they plan to bring the pain to a new generation.

WWE unveiled the Women's Tag Team Titles in February 2019. Inside the brutal Elimination Chamber, The Boss & Hug Connection made history by outlasting five teams to become the inaugural champs. Weeks later, WWE Hall of Famer Beth Phoenix came out of retirement to pair with her ally Natalya. As tensions mounted, two other teams proved worthy of joining the fray. So, a Fatal 4-Way Match was scheduled, setting the odds firmly against the reigning champs.

WrestleMania WOMEN'S TAG TEAM CHAMPIONSHIP MATCH

ACTION

FATAL 4-WAY MATCH
FOR THE WWE WOMEN'S TAG TEAM CHAMPIONSHIP

SASHA BANKS & BAYLEY VS NIA JAX & TAMINA VS THE IICONICS VS NATALYA & BETH PHOENIX

RIGHT AWAY, TEAMS GANG UP AND EJECT THE IMPOSING NIA JAX FROM THE RING. SMART STRATEGY!

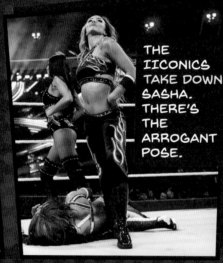

THE IICONICS TAKE DOWN SASHA. THERE'S THE ARROGANT POSE.

BUT THERE'S BETH PHOENIX WITH AMAZING STRENGTH! NOT SO SMUG NOW, ARE THEY?

BAYLEY DISRUPTS THE PINFALL ATTEMPT IN THE NICK OF TIME.

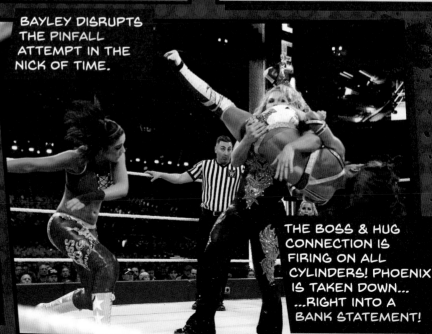

NATALYA AND PHOENIX WITH A HART ATTACK. THE ANVIL WOULD BE PROUD!

THE BOSS & HUG CONNECTION IS FIRING ON ALL CYLINDERS! PHOENIX IS TAKEN DOWN... ...RIGHT INTO A BANK STATEMENT!

BETH ESCAPES, AND NOW NATALYA WITH A STATEMENT OF HER OWN, A DOUBLE SHARPSHOOTER!

TAMINA AND JAX ARE BACK IN THE SCRUM, AND SHOWING WHY THEY ARE CALLED THE SAMOAN SLAUGHTERHOUSE!

AND THEN BACK IN THE RING, SO DOES BAYLEY! BUT PHOENIX RECOVERS AND...

UNBELIEVABLE! A GLAM SLAM FROM THE TOP ROPE!

THE ACTION SPILLS TO THE OUTSIDE. SASHA TAKES TO THE AIR!

THE HALL OF FAMER HAS BAYLEY PINNED, BUT ROYCE SWOOPS IN AND SPOILS IT...

...AND BILLIE KAY STEALS THE EASY PIN. THE IICONICS ARE YOUR NEW CHAMPS!

THIS CROWD IS STUNNED, AND FROM THE LOOKS OF THEM, SO ARE THE IICONICS!

21

SMACKDOWN
20 YEARS & COUNTING

It has been 20 riotous years since **The Rock** raised his eyebrow to the sky and promised to "lay the smackdown," inspiring the name for a new flagship show to rival Monday Night Raw. Now, SmackDown is all grown up, and we've rolled out the blue carpet for a 20 year anniversary bonanza, starting with a stroll down memory lane!

NOVEMBER 11, 1999

BIG BLUE DEBUTS

Many Superstars' first steps in a WWE ring were between the blue ropes. Check out these future stars during their younger days!

The Game Terminated

The baddest man in WWE, Stone Cold Steve Austin, and the baddest man in the movies, Arnold Schwarzenegger, joined forces to take down Triple H!

Opportunity Strikes
MAY 11, 2007

Sometimes to reach new heights, Superstars will stoop to new lows, none more than Edge. He invented the Money in the Bank cash-in on a defenceless opponent and even married **SmackDown** GM Vicki Guerrero to shift the odds in his favour.

A Seismic Superplex
JUNE 12, 2003

A Superplex by Brock Lesnar to Big Show crushed the ring to smithereens!

APRIL 7, 2005

Cena's Time is Now

Bald Medalist
MAY 23 2002

After losing a Hair vs Hair Match, Kurt Angle covered his chrome dome with a ridiculous wig. Two years later, he used his own shears on Big Show! How did he keep the giant still? With a tranquilizer dart, of course!

SmackDown was where The Doctor of Thuganomics evolved into The Champ! The rapping Superstar won his first WWE Championship and unveiled a flashy new title with a spinning logo. It was Cena's first of 16 World Titles, and it all began on SmackDown.

Hopeless Romantics

Unfortunately for Edge, weddings on **SmackDown** end as well as they do on **Raw** - horribly! Edge's bride caught him smooching the wedding planner, Alicia Fox!

THE SMACKDOWN FIST!

This fiery fist jutted from the **SmackDown** set from 2001-2008. It was 17 feet long, 12 feet wide and weighed 6000 lbs! That is over 1000 lbs heavier than a London Black Cab!

Randy Orton
April 25, 2002
(22 years old)

John Cena
June 27, 2002
(25 years old)

Batista
May 9, 2002
(33 years old)

Rey Mysterio
July 25, 2002
(27 years old)

Bobby Lashley
September 25, 2005
(29 years old)

Drew McIntyre
October 12, 2007
(22 years old)

The Bellas
November 7, 2008
(24 years old)

Jinder Mahal
April 29, 2011
(24 years old)

Ballin'!

SmackDown's highest paid free agent, MVP, lived up to his contract as United States Champion, holding the title for 342 days from 2007-2008.

Brother's Destruction
OCTOBER 22, 2010

As Kane threatened the mystery Superstar who brutalized Undertaker, Undertaker revealed the assailant to be Kane himself! The Brothers of Destruction once again became bitter enemies.

Champ That Runs the Camp
NOVEMBER 7, 2017

In 2017, AJ Styles defeated Jinder Mahal in Manchester, England. The win made AJ the first Superstar to win the WWE Championship in the UK in the title's 54-year history.

Thanksgiving Food Fights!

SmackDown's annual American feast always ends with party guests being doused with gravy and other flying fixin's. Never imitate Superstars' moves... or their table manners!

Brand Supremacy

SmackDown bested **Raw** to win the first Bragging Rights Trophy in 2009, and then again in 2010.

SMACKDOWN
20 YEARS & COUNTING
SMACKDOWN STANDOUTS

UNDERTAKER

From: Death Valley
Height: 6' 10"
Weight: 309 lbs
Signature Moves:
Tombstone, Chokeslam,
Old School, Hells Gate,
Snake Eyes

Undertaker's shadow has loomed over **SmackDown** for nearly its entire history. When Kane buried him alive in 2003, he returned to WWE scarier than ever! He became **SmackDown's** Grim Reaper, ready to dig holes and take souls at a moment's notice. Even now, the toll of his bell freezes his foes in terror!

EDDIE GUERRERO

From: El Paso, TX
Height: 5' 10"
Weight: 220 lbs
Signature Moves:
Frog Splash,
Three Amigos

Nobody loves a Superstar who lies, cheats and steals...unless that Superstar is Eddie Guerrero. Eddie grew up in a sports entertainment family. He followed his dream all the way to becoming WWE Champion in 2004. Though he bent the rules a little bit (ok, a lot), he was too charming to root against!

THE ROCK

From: Miami, FL
Height: 6' 3"
Weight: 260 lbs
Signature Moves:
Rock Bottom,
Peoples Elbow

Not only did The Rock coin the term "smackdown," he spent the show's early days laying one down on the evil McMahon-Helmsley faction. The Great One always kept the blue brand electrifying. Naturally, **SmackDown** selected him as the first overall pick in the inaugural WWE Draft.

JBL

From: New York City
Height: 6' 6"
Weight: 290 lbs
Signature Move:
Clothesline From Hell

With his stretch white limo and ten gallon cowboy hats, this loudmouth tycoon was untouchable for 280 days as WWE Champion. His personal goon squad called "The Cabinet" protected his title reign. As his victories mounted, he taunted the WWE Universe, calling himself a "Wrestling God!"

REY MYSTERIO

From: San Diego, CA
Height: 5' 6"
Weight: 175 lbs
Signature Moves:
619, West Coast Pop

Often called "The Biggest Little Man," Rey Mysterio proved the only size that matters is the size of one's heart. Rey befuddled bigger foes by defying the laws of gravity. The masked Superstar's 619 finisher, where he whips his legs in a full circle between the ropes, still dazzles the WWE Universe today!

KURT ANGLE

From: Pittsburgh, PA
Height: 6'
Weight: 220 lbs
Signature Moves:
Angle Slam, Ankle Lock

This gifted athlete sported a shiny gold medal around his neck that he won as an amateur wrestler. Making the leap to WWE, he never missed a beat. Angle dissected his opponents' moves with superior skill between the ropes, not to mention his three I's – Integrity. Intensity. Intelligence.

KING BOOKER

From: Houston, TX
Height: 6' 3"
Weight: 256 lbs
Signature Moves: Bookend, Spin-a-roonie

When Booker T won the 2006 King of the Ring tournament, he took the throne as King Booker. Donning a flowing red cape, shimmering crown and wielding a sceptre, this regal Superstar ruled **SmackDown** with an iron fist. He even forced other Superstars to kiss his feet! All hail King Booker!

NATALYA

From: Calgary, Alberta, Canada
Height: 5' 5"
Signature Move: Sharpshooter

The daughter of Jim "The Anvil" Neidhart has been a WWE stalwart for over a decade. During her career, women's competition in WWE has ramped up to a fever pitch. Through it all, "Nattie" has been the one constant, inspiring others to raise their game, or get wrenched into the Hart family's Sharpshooter!

RANDY ORTON

From: St. Louis, MO
Height: 6' 5"
Weight: 260 lbs
Signature Move: RKO

When this third-generation Superstar returned to **SmackDown** in 2005, he quickly dealt an RKO to Undertaker out of nowhere. That set the tone for the next fifteen years. No one knows what goes through Orton's reptilian mind. The only thing predictable about him is his complete and utter lack of mercy.

EVE

From: Denver, CO
Height: 5' 8"
Signature Move: Moonsault

A former dancer trained in jiu-jitsu, Eve had the athletic tools to succeed, but her greatest weapon might have been her mind. She won three Divas Championships, competing with the likes of Beth Phoenix, Natalya and Nikki Bella. Then she quickly rose to power as an Assistant General Manager of **SmackDown**.

THE USOS

From: San Francisco, CA
Height: Jey 6'2", Jimmy 6'3"
Weight: Jey 228 lbs, Jimmy 251 lbs

Though drafted to Raw in 2019, these twins built their impressive legacy on **SmackDown** from day one (ish). For a decade, they've made their Samoan ancestors proud, collecting five Tag Team Championships. With a blend of high flying ability and streetwise grit, they still keep WWE's tag team ranks on lock down!

AJ STYLES

From: Gainesville, GA
Height: 5' 11"
Weight: 218 lbs
Signature Moves: Phenomenal Forearm, Calf Crusher

Before moving to **Raw**, AJ spent four years molding **SmackDown** into "The House that AJ Styles Built." He held the WWE Championship for 371 days, the longest reign in six years, displaying unrivalled ability between the ropes (and above them). There is only one word to describe AJ- phenomenal.

SMACKDOWN
20 YEARS & COUNTING
SEARCH-A-WORD

I'm hiding in here somewhere. Come find me and some of your favorite SmackDown memories, if you dare!

```
N B Y G R Y U L V O R N V G U A G H E W
O L A G D F S A N F K F H U I B L C R A
I U D G L H M N X O J C R W O L A S T L
P E W A S J K D R M H C O L C E Q E K C
M B E S N V U O W R B A Q R P A D B F F
A R N L U Q O F S K T O M N E D Y E D P
H A O Z E X C O Y U S L I C Y H D W E B
C N I F X J G P D M N T Z L M P T O S V
E D T C A T V P Q M S D Q Q P E P I Q T
W W B W R I D O O E F N E G Z L N H G M
W M P E O G R R R E G F I R E K H A D B
X D W F V L X T K K J J T S T M H O H R
S Y W D H O E U Z S L G E Q X A U T W S
L M W D G Q T N S K Z Y U N B P K I C B
Y M J E H F H I N N E S G G Q U C E W U
R O N H C W S T S B L Q L U M R A B R B
I A F O U Q G Y R B E C K Y L Y N C H R
K T Z Q M T W O K C A M S G N I K L A T
N T P U U B W N A M Y E G O O B N R H F
R S C V W C B I I D X Y X K N G A I D Q
```

WWE Champion
Peoples Eyebrow
The Rock
Blue Brand

Teddy Long
Land of Opportunity
Becky Lynch

Undertaker
Talking Smack
Boogeyman

Kane
Shane McMahon
New Day
Rest in Peace

SMACKDOWN SUPERSTARS TO WATCH

ALEISTER BLACK

This brooding Superstar first emerged in NXT, where he dominated for nearly two years, enjoying a reign as NXT Champion. If his gothic entrance isn't enough to give opponents the creeps, the thought of his explosive martial arts kicks sure will. Black and Ricochet made life tough for WWE's tag team division before splitting. With only his gloomy thoughts for company, he is even scarier!

ANDRADE

A former NXT Champion, Andrade has all the makings of WWE's next great luchador, and he knows it too! Never lacking in confidence, Andrade backs up his tough talk with blinding speed and striking athleticism. With his feisty associate, Zelina Vega, by his side, he's scored impressive wins in his first year on **SmackDown**, and is poised to reach greater heights.

ASUKA

She might be called "The Empress of Tomorrow" but Asuka's time to shine is today. Boasting "no one is ready for Asuka," she began her WWE career by going undefeated for a whopping 523 days and winning the first-ever Women's Royal Rumble. Asuka claimed her first **SmackDown** Women's Championship in the first-ever Women's TLC Match, and is only beginning to make history in WWE.

KEVIN OWENS

This burly brawler does not make a great friend. Just ask Sami Zayn, Chris Jericho and most recently, The New Day, who he has brutally double-crossed. Owens can be trusted to do one thing – fight anyone! Lucky for him, he is one of the best at it. He has battled and badmouthed his way to Universal, Intercontinental and United States Championships, and even stirred things up with his own talk show- "The Kevin Owens Show."

SHINSUKE NAKAMURA

Hailed as "The King of Strong Style," Shinsuke is notorious for his swift and harsh offensive strikes. For the past four years, WWE Superstars have learned first-hand what made him a sensation in his home country of Japan. Recently, he's adopted a Rockstar swagger, becoming even more flashy and unpredictable in the ring, which is

LARS SULLIVAN

This enraged lunatic seems bent on demolishing everything in sight. With his freakish abilities, who can stop him? His fists resemble the head of an oversized mallet and the body they are attached to appears carved from stone. Sullivan doesn't say much, but his purpose is clear – to punish his WWE foes, and enjoy every moment of it.

DID YOU KNOW?

WHAT FORMER WCW CHAMPION NICKNAMED "THE MASTADON"

MEGA MOVES

WWE Superstars always save one **lights-out manoeuvre** to end a match in an instant, whether **spinning through the air** like me or **squeezing a foe into submission** like Samoa Joe. Can you match the Superstars below with their **fantastic finishers**?

MOVES

A CAPTAIN'S HOOK
B DDT

C COQUINA CLUTCH

D ECLIPSE

E END OF DAYS
F MOONSAULT
G 630 SPLASH
H PTO
I PURPLE RAINMAKER
J ZIG ZAG

1 BARON CORBIN

2 RICOCHET

3 DOLPH ZIGGLER

5 EMBER MOON

4 THE BRIAN KENDRICK

6 PAIGE

7 JAKE "THE SNAKE" ROBERTS

8 SAMOA JOE

9 LITA

10 VELVETEEN DREAM

Answers on pages 76-77

28

SIGNATURE MOVE
GENERATOR

Having trouble naming your **own** WWE **finishing move**? Perhaps the DIY method doesn't work for you. **To help** you along, I've put together this **helpful generator**.

BIRTH MONTH

January	Spinning
~~February~~	~~Leaping~~
March	Irish
April	Colossal
May	Sabre-toothed
June	Mutant
~~July~~	~~Royal~~
August	Montezuma's
September	Flailing
October	Thirsty
November	Juggling
December	Charging

FIRST INITIAL

A	Mud
B	Porcupine
C	Rubbish
D	Armpit
E	Dragon
F	Broccoli
G	Phantom
H	Jockey
I	Martian
J	Rhinoceros
K	Yo-yo
L	Sponge
M	Sceptre
N	Ping Pong
O	Chainsaw
P	Vuvuzela
Q	Spaghetti
R	Diaper
S	Garden gnome
T	Belly button
U	Trash can
V	Icicle
W	Toe nail
X	Pimple
Y	Knick knack
Z	Hashtag

SECOND INITIAL

A	Chest
B	Crawl
C	Shuffle
D	Kick
E	Finale
F	Tango
G	Revenge
H	Lunge
I	Shimmy
J	Blitz
K	Stomp
L	Smash
M	Charmer
N	Destroyer
O	Slap
P	Plunge
Q	Massacre
R	Twirl
S	Blaster
T	Boogaloo
U	Rocket
V	Crusher
W	Clutch
X	Mixer
Y	Belch
Z	Slam

MY FINISHING MOVE IS THE

Phantom Clutch Kick

WRESTLEMANIA FALLS COUNT ANYWHERE MATCH

BACKGROUND

THE COMPETITORS

In his long career, this "A-list" Superstar has racked up an **impressive slate** of both championship wins and Hollywood credits. If The Miz is in town, a **must-see event** is about to take place! He and his lovely wife, Maryse, star in the hit reality show *Miz & Mrs*, which documents their chaotic lives in the public eye. Through all the glitz and red carpets, the outspoken Miz keeps **building on his success**. Only Chris Jericho has won more Intercontinental Championships in all of WWE history. As a tag team Superstar, Miz has won titles with five different partners, including...

THE MIZ

THE BUILD-UP...

VS SHANE MCMAHON

When Shane subbed in for The Miz to win the finals of **WWE's Best in the World Tournament**, the odd pair decided to tag together. The newfound **"Co-Besties"** clicked in the ring, winning the SmackDown Tag Team Championships at Royal Rumble 2019. Their newfound success delighted Miz's father, who cheered his son from ringside. The feelgood story ended, however, when Shane coldly attacked both Miz and Mr. Miz. No titles were on the line when the former friends met at *WrestleMania*. **This one was personal.**

WRESTLEMANIA FALLS COUNT ANYWHERE MATCH

ACTION THE MIZ VS SHANE MCMAHON

SHANE IS BERATING THE ANNOUNCER AND DEMANDING A BETTER INTRODUCTION. AS THE MIZ USED TO SAY, REALLY?

NOW, SHANE WASTES NO TIME ATTACKING MIZ. HE GRABS HIS FACE, JUST LIKE HE DID TO MIZ'S POOR OLD POPS!

WITH MIZ LAID OUT, SHANE IS LOOKING TO PUT THIS MATCH AWAY BUT MR. MIZ BLOCKS HIS PATH!

IT'S A FALLS COUNT ANYWHERE MATCH, AND MIZ PLANS TO USE THE ENTIRE STADIUM.

THE ELDER MIZ WANTS A PIECE OF SHANE, BUT FIRST, SHANE SHOWS HIM A PROPER FIGHTING STANCE.

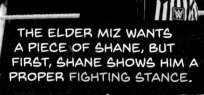

HE SWINGS FROM TWO CABLES AND BLASTS SHANE WITH A KICK!

THE MIZ HAS SEEN ENOUGH. SHANE HAS PUT HIS HANDS ON HIS DAD FOR THE LAST TIME!

THE INTERNATIONAL ANNOUNCERS' TABLES TAKE A BEATING IN THE MELEE.

UP ON THE SCAFFOLDING, MIZ DELIVERS A SKULL CRUSHING FINALE! HE'S TAKEN OVER THIS MATCH!

A FITTING REVENGE! MIZ WITH THE FACE GRAB! WHAT DOES HE HAVE IN MIND? THAT SCAFFOLDING IS 15 FEET HIGH. HE CAN'T POSSIBLY...

OH

MY

GOD!!

BUT SHANE LANDED ON THE MIZ. IN A FALLS COUNT ANYWHERE MATCH, THAT'S A LEGAL PINFALL! SHANE WAS DECIMATED IN THIS MATCH, BUT UNWITTINGLY STEALS THE VICTORY! SOMETHING TELLS ME THIS RIVALRY IS FAR FROM OVER.

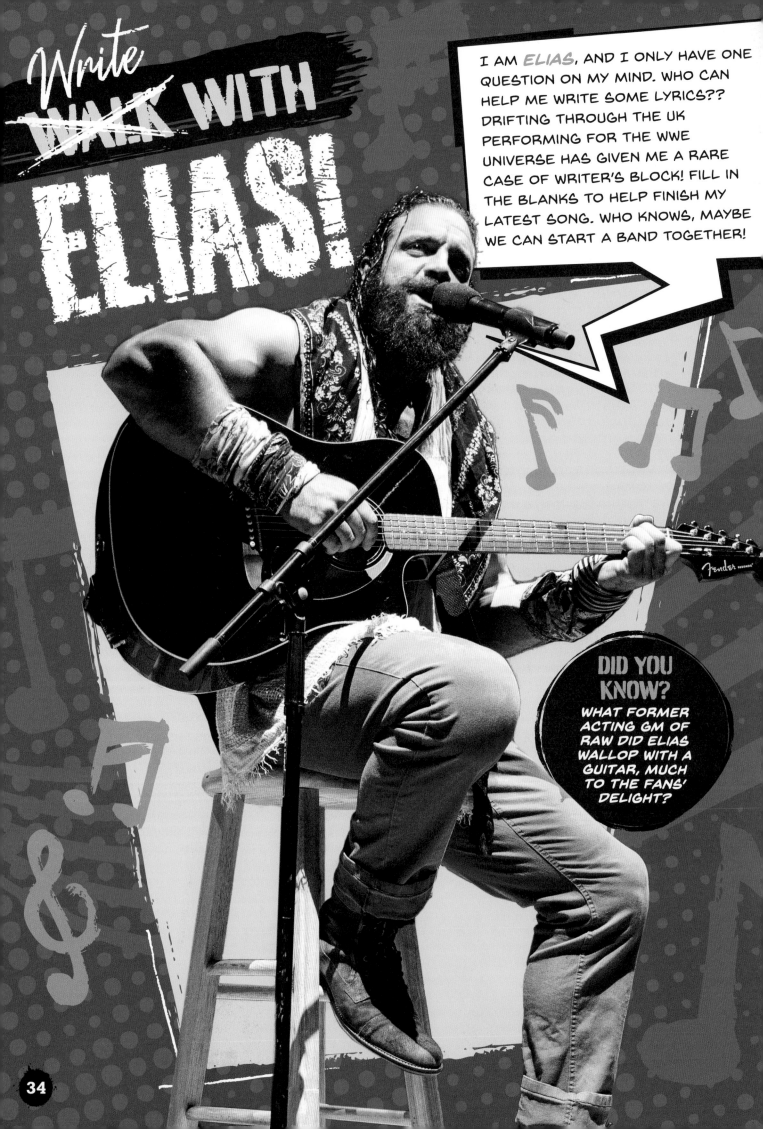

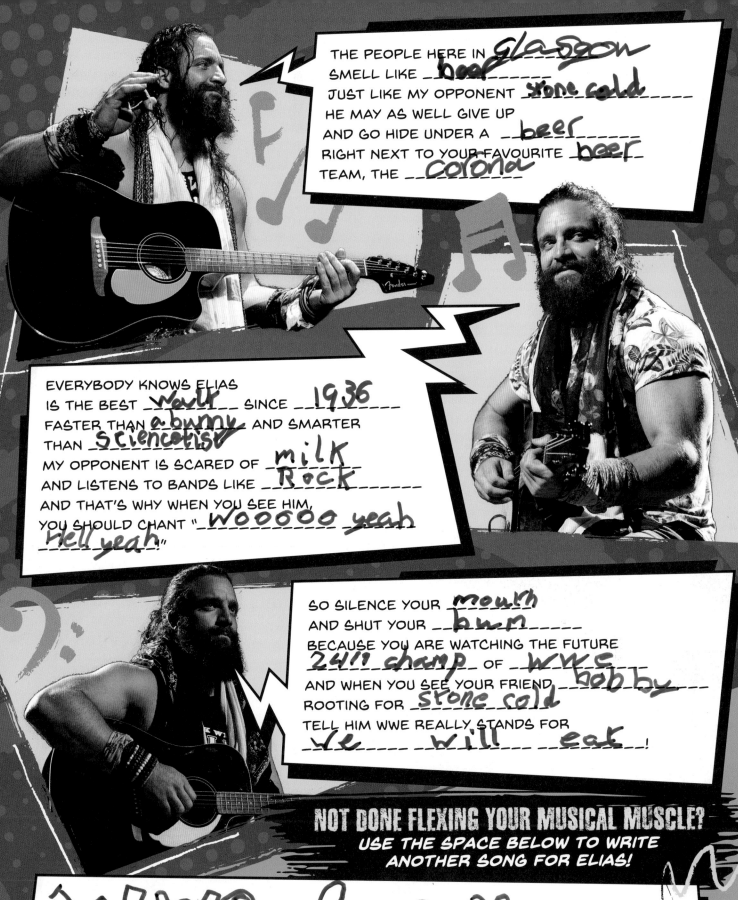

TRUTH OR FALSE

WHAT'S UP?? SAY, CARMELLA, HOW ABOUT A LITTLE...

DANCE BREAK?

YOU READ MY MIND! DANCE BREAK!

WAIT...THIS BOOK DOESN'T PLAY MUSIC.

I JUST SAW ELIAS PLAYING THE GUITAR ON THE PREVIOUS PAGE!

THAT'S *TRUE* BUT, *HEY!*, YOU KNOW WHAT WOULD BE *FABULOUS*? A GAME OF TRUE OR FALSE.

HOW DO YOU PLAY?

WELL, IF I SAY, "I WON THE FIRST-EVER WOMEN'S MONEY IN THE BANK," YOU WOULD SAY THE ANSWER IS...

...C?

NEVER MIND, JUST START SAYING STUFF, AND LET THE WWE UNIVERSE GUESS WHETHER IT'S TRUE OR FALSE..

DID YOU KNOW?
WHO WAS R-TRUTH'S PARTNER IN THE AWESOME TRUTH?

1 I had an imaginary friend name Little Joey
T ⚪ F ⚪

2 I had a real friend named James Ellsworth
T ⚪ F ⚪

3 I was once a Tag Team Champion with Kofi Kingston
T ⚪ F ⚪

4 I once managed a tag team in NXT
T ⚪ F ⚪

5 I won the LOL Moment of the Year Award for thinking I was in the Money in the Bank Ladder Match, when I wasn't
T ⚪ F ⚪

6 I won Money in the Bank... twice
T ⚪ F ⚪

7 I'm from Truth or Consequences, New Mexico
T ⚪ F ⚪

8 I'm from The Bronx, New York City
T ⚪ F ⚪

9 I brought back John Cena's Intercontinental Championship Open Challenge
T ⚪ F ⚪

10 I brought back the moonwalk!
T ⚪ F ⚪

ANSWER: THE MIZ!

Answers on pages 76-77

36

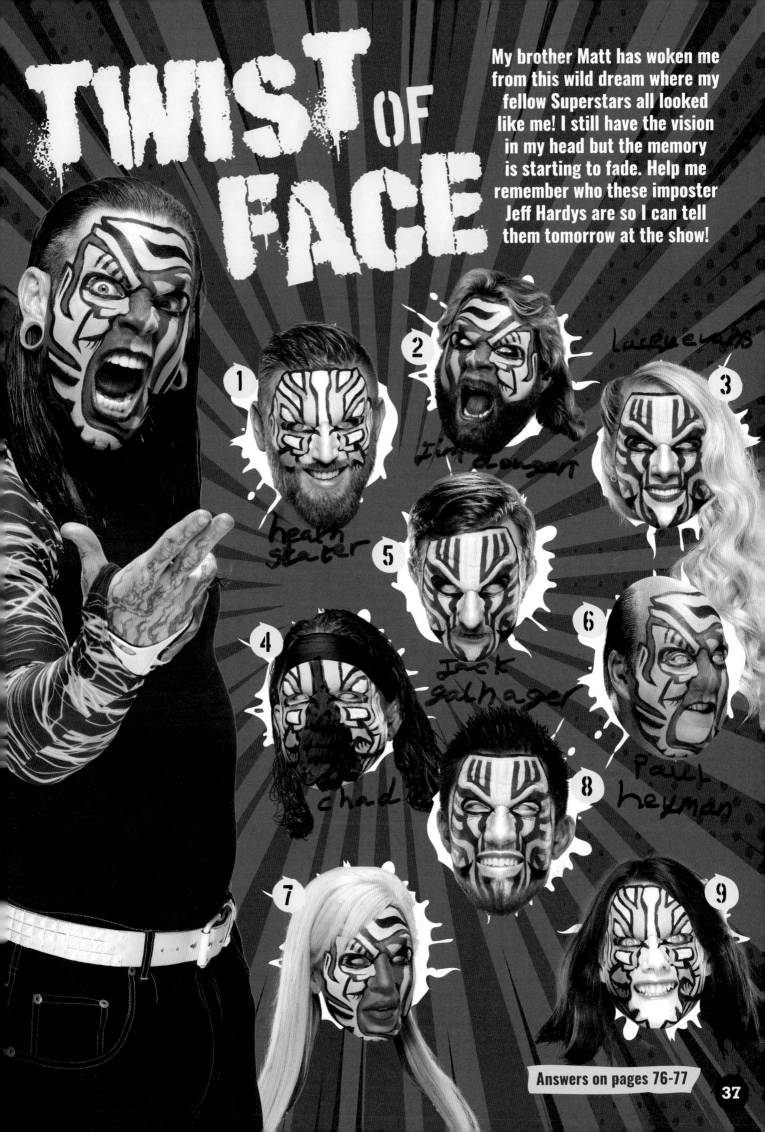

TWIST OF FACE

My brother Matt has woken me from this wild dream where my fellow Superstars all looked like me! I still have the vision in my head but the memory is starting to fade. Help me remember who these imposter Jeff Hardys are so I can tell them tomorrow at the show!

1 — heath slater

2 — Tim clougan

3 — Lacey evans

4 — chad

5 — Jack gallagher

6

7

8 — Paul heyman

9

Answers on pages 76-77

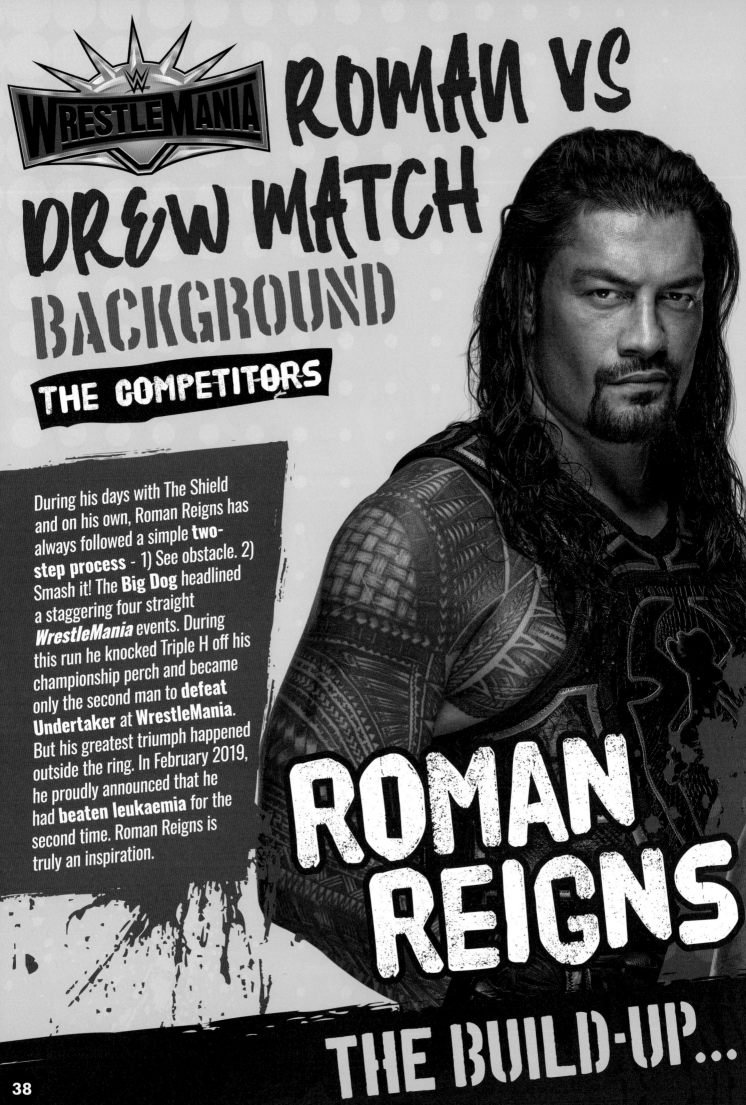

WRESTLEMANIA ROMAN VS DREW MATCH BACKGROUND

THE COMPETITORS

During his days with The Shield and on his own, Roman Reigns has always followed a simple **two-step process** - 1) See obstacle. 2) Smash it! The **Big Dog** headlined a staggering four straight *WrestleMania* events. During this run he knocked Triple H off his championship perch and became only the second man to **defeat Undertaker** at WrestleMania. But his greatest triumph happened outside the ring. In February 2019, he proudly announced that he had **beaten leukaemia** for the second time. Roman Reigns is truly an inspiration.

ROMAN REIGNS

THE BUILD-UP...

If there is a hint of remorse behind his icy glare, The **Scottish Psychopath** has not shown it. After an uneven first run with WWE, McIntyre returned in 2017 with a purpose. For the past two years, this towering, grizzled brute has **strong-armed** his way into the main event scene. With his intimidating look, devastating Claymore Kick and **disdain for all living beings** in his path, there is no telling the **destruction** Drew will cause or who he will target next.

VS DREW MCINTYRE

"I'm in remission!" In three words, Roman Reigns delivered perhaps the greatest news ever spoken inside a WWE ring. Having overcome a scary **bout of leukaemia** once again, Roman focused on **resuming his dream** inside a WWE ring. While the WWE Universe rejoiced, one man was bent on turning Roman's dream into a nightmare, Drew McIntyre. After a series of **callous attacks** by McIntyre, doubt was cast on Roman's ability to compete. But no one doubts Roman Reigns in his own yard! If **McIntyre wanted a fight**, he would get it!

WRESTLEMANIA ROMAN VS DREW MATCH

ACTION ROMAN REIGNS VS DREW MCINTYRE

ROMAN REIGNS HAS SAID HE WOULD NOT BE HERE IF NOT FOR THE WWE UNIVERSE. THEY ARE READY TO SEE THEIR HERO TONIGHT!

MCINTYRE IS A REMORSELESS BEHEMOTH OF A SUPERSTAR, BUT THE BIG DOG AIN'T BACKING DOWN.

THE BELL HAS RUNG AND BOTH MEN ARE THROWING FURIOUS FISTS. THIS WILL BE AN EMOTIONAL FIGHT. WHOEVER CAN CONTROL THE PACE WILL COME OUT ON TOP.

THE BIG DOG GETS THE FIRST BITE WITH A SAMOAN DROP! HE HASN'T MISSED A BEAT!

BUT MCINTYRE GETS HIM IN HIS CLUTCHES FOR A SPINEBUSTER!

THE IMPACT HAS WEAKENED REIGNS. DREW POUNCES! THE SINISTER SCOT IS IMPLORING ROMAN TO GIVE IT UP NOW...

...BUT ROMAN FIGHTS OUT OF IT AND HURLS DREW TO THE OUTSIDE!

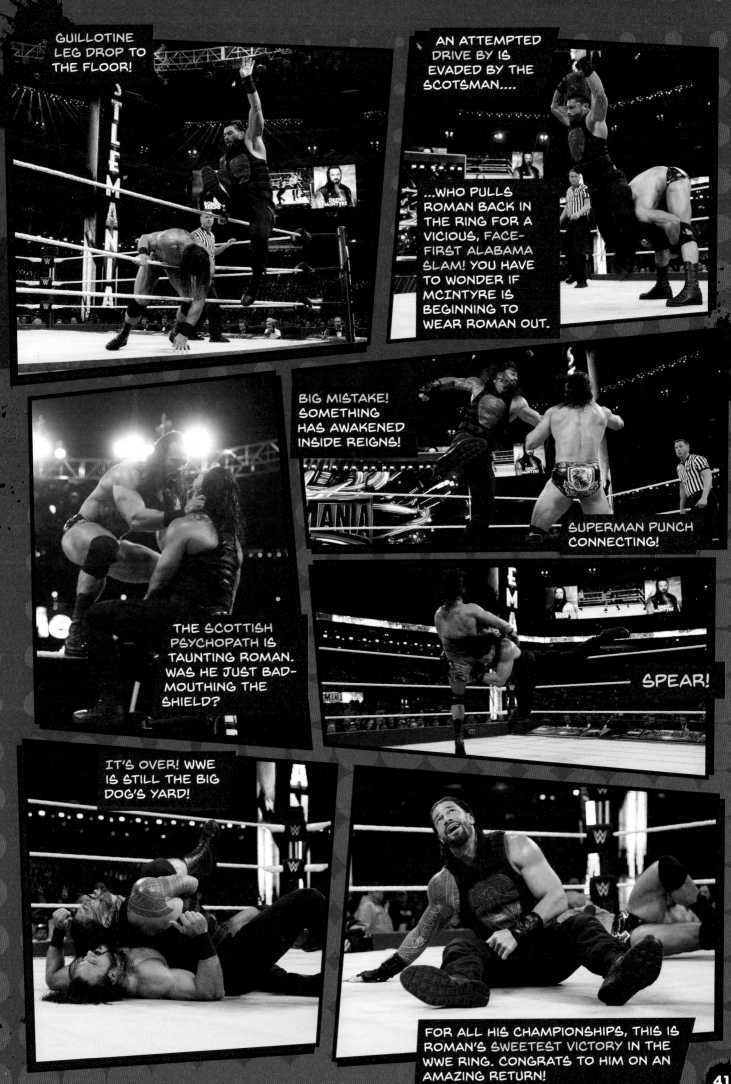

GUILLOTINE LEG DROP TO THE FLOOR!

AN ATTEMPTED DRIVE BY IS EVADED BY THE SCOTSMAN....

...WHO PULLS ROMAN BACK IN THE RING FOR A VICIOUS, FACE-FIRST ALABAMA SLAM! YOU HAVE TO WONDER IF MCINTYRE IS BEGINNING TO WEAR ROMAN OUT.

BIG MISTAKE! SOMETHING HAS AWAKENED INSIDE REIGNS!

SUPERMAN PUNCH CONNECTING!

THE SCOTTISH PSYCHOPATH IS TAUNTING ROMAN. WAS HE JUST BAD-MOUTHING THE SHIELD?

SPEAR!

IT'S OVER! WWE IS STILL THE BIG DOG'S YARD!

FOR ALL HIS CHAMPIONSHIPS, THIS IS ROMAN'S SWEETEST VICTORY IN THE WWE RING. CONGRATS TO HIM ON AN AMAZING RETURN!

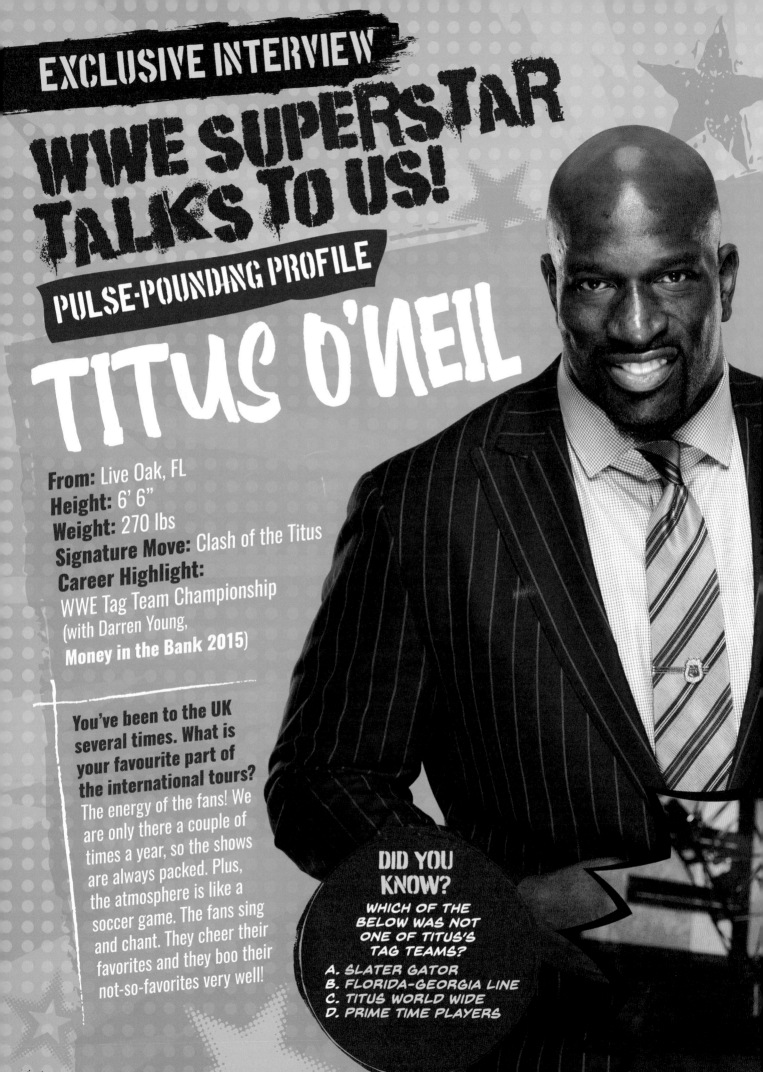

WWE SUPERSTAR TALKS TO US!

PULSE-POUNDING PROFILE

TITUS O'NEIL

From: Live Oak, FL
Height: 6' 6"
Weight: 270 lbs
Signature Move: Clash of the Titus
Career Highlight:
WWE Tag Team Championship
(with Darren Young,
Money in the Bank 2015)

You've been to the UK several times. What is your favourite part of the international tours?
The energy of the fans! We are only there a couple of times a year, so the shows are always packed. Plus, the atmosphere is like a soccer game. The fans sing and chant. They cheer their favorites and they boo their not-so-favorites very well!

DID YOU KNOW?
WHICH OF THE BELOW WAS NOT ONE OF TITUS'S TAG TEAMS?
A. SLATER GATOR
B. FLORIDA-GEORGIA LINE
C. TITUS WORLD WIDE
D. PRIME TIME PLAYERS

ANSWER: B. FLORIDA-GEORGIA LINE

In your new book, you talk about your love of food. Have you tried anything new or exotic recently?
Recently I've grown fond of octopus and eel. It was scary to try at first but now I look for it everywhere I go. It goes to show you the benefits of getting over your fears. I also got over my fear of heights recently. I went down the world's largest slide at the ArcelorMittal Orbit in London's Olympic Park. Because of that, I was able to ride a roller coaster for the first time.

In the book, you discuss your fear of snakes. Have you confronted that fear as well?
Yes. When I was in college, my roommate brought home a pet snake! So not only did I confront the fear, I ended up being part owner of a snake.

When not in the ring, you are often seen wearing a suit. Why is keeping a professional appearance so important?
The famous American athlete Deion Sanders once said, "If you look good, you play good." I've adopted that mentality. Dressing the way I do shows confidence, which creates opportunity. Also, I grew up poor and couldn't afford nice clothes. Now, I am able to use fashion to build my persona in and out of the ring.

Are there any WWE Legends you grew up watching that you've tried to be like in WWE?
I loved Junkyard Dog. He was beloved during a time when diversity was not as celebrated. I also loved The Rock's energy and creativity. I try to be a combination of those two – electrifying when I need to be and someone who is loved by people of all backgrounds for the person that I am.

Do you have any special pre-match rituals that help get you ready to compete?
I wear the same orange and blue Florida Gators socks under my boots every match. That is the one superstitious thing that I do.

If you were not a WWE Superstar, what career would you have pursued?
Coaching American football. That is what I planned to do before I took the adventurous walk through the backdoors of Florida Championship Wrestling, which became NXT.

Do you have aspirations of joining your good friend Batista in the Marvel Universe or getting into Hollywood?
Not just aspirations but I am taking steps toward doing so. I've always wanted to be in TV or film. I think it will happen in the very near future.

If you were a superhero, what would your superpower be?
Being able to take the angriest people and turning them into the nicest people on earth!

After you stumbled and fell under the ring in Saudi Arabia, you did a great job turning the mishap into a positive moment. What is the lesson there for younger fans?
The lesson is simple. Everybody falls down and makes mistakes. The way you respond to mistakes is what people remember the most. Don't be afraid to stumble in life, because all that matters is how you get up and keep going!

In your book, you talk about wanting to create a school. What was your favorite school subject?
My favorites have always been History and English, and still are to this day. My least favorite- Math!

What was your favorite book?
Like a lot of kids, my favorite was Dr. Seuss's **The Cat in the Hat**.

THERE'S
NO SUCH THING
AS A
BAD KID

How I Went from Stereotype to Prototype

W TITUS O'NEIL

Thanks to Titus for stopping by to chat! Be sure to check out his new book, **There's No Such Thing As A Bad Kid!**

ALEXA-GRAMS

Were you surprised when WWE named yours truly the host of *WrestleMania*? I wasn't. When you are a star of my calibre, people listen when you speak. That is, unless your words get all jumbled up! Make yourself useful and unscramble the words below. Hint: They all pertain to me (of course!)

1 DEWITTS

2 MUCUSLOB

3 GOSSEDD

4 UFRY

5 EMTOMN FO SLIBS

6 CEOEFF

7 PASTURERS

8 MACHONIP

9 UNOLOVEIT

10 IFEV TEFE

DID YOU KNOW? Alexa Bliss was the first Superstar to win both the *RAW* and *SmackDown* Women's Championships. Who was the second?

ANSWER: CHARLOTTE FLAIR

Answers on pages 76-77

CRUISERWEIGHT CROSSWORD

WWE 205 LIVE

The athletes of 205 Live deliver the most exciting hour on television each week! Show me how much you know about the unrivalled athletes of the Purple Brand by tackling this tricky crossword puzzle.

ACROSS

3 Masked trio _____ House Party
4 Cedric Alexander move
6 Buddy Murphy's home
10 Last name of Mike and Maria

DOWN

1 Prefers a 'no fly zone'
2 Gentleman Jack Gallagher prop
5 Commentator Nigel _____
7 High flying hype man for Bobby Lashley
8 Ariya Daivari nickname – Persian _____
9 Lasted 30 minutes in the 2019 Royal Rumble

Answers on pages 76-77

WWE LEGENDS QUIZ

Wooooo! If John Cena can host a quiz in this book, then so can the original 16-time World Champ! I used to say "diamonds are forever", well, so are the WWE Legends. So stay sharp on your WWE history. You never know when the Nature Boy will appear with 16 more mind-bending trivia questions.

1 What did "Million Dollar Man" Ted DiBiase and Irwin R. Schyster name their tag team?

- **A** Big & Rich ☐
- **B** The Aristocrats ☐
- **C** The Corporation ☐
- **D** Money Inc ☑

2 Which was NOT one of Shawn Michaels' nicknames?

- **A** The Showstopper ☐
- **B** The Excellence of Execution ☑
- **C** The Heartbreak Kid ☐
- **D** The Main Event ☐

3 Where was Ultimate Warrior from?

- **A** Venice Beach, California ☐
- **B** Stone Mountain, Georgia ☐
- **C** Parts Unknown ☑
- **D** Grenoble in the French Alps ☐

4 Who used his massive rump to perform a move called The Stinkface?

- **A** Rikishi ☑
- **B** Earthquake ☐
- **C** Bastion Booger ☐
- **D** Yokozuna ☐

5 What WWE Hall of Famer is The Rock's dad?

- **A** Mr. T ☐
- **B** Rocky Johnson ☑
- **C** Tony Atlas ☐
- **D** Sika ☐

6 Who is this Legend who once fought crime alongside The Hurricane?

- **A** Molly Holly ☑
- **B** Trish Stratus ☐
- **C** Victoria ☐
- **D** Marlena ☐

7 Who returned to help Team WWE battle The Nexus at *SummerSlam 2010*?

- **A** Jim "The Anvil" Neidhart ☐
- **B** Jimmy Hart ☐
- **C** "Dangerous" Danny Davis ☐
- **D** Bret "Hit Man" Hart ☑

8 What multi-time Tag Team Champions enjoyed a goofy "5 Second Pose" for fans to snap photos?

- **A** The Dudley Boyz ☐
- **B** Edge & Christian ☑
- **C** The Oddities ☐
- **D** The APA ☐

9 Who won the first-ever Royal Rumble Match?

A "Hacksaw" Jim Duggan ☐
B Junkyard Dog ☐
C Roddy Piper ☐
D Hulk Hogan ☑

10 Who used his strength to pull two tractor trailer trucks on an episode of *SmackDown*?

A The Rock ☐
B Big Show ☐
C Kane ☐
D Mark Henry ☑

11 Who is this WCW icon who shockingly attacked Triple H at *Survivor Series 2014*?

A Diamond Dallas Page ☐
B Great Muta ☐
C Sting ☑
D Goldberg ☐

12 Kairi Sane won the first annual WWE women's tournament, named after which Hall of Famer?

A Mae Young ☑
B Sensational Sherri ☐
C Chyna ☐
D Wendi Richter ☐

13 This gear worn by Sasha Banks at *WrestleMania 32* was inspired by which of her WWE heroes?

A Mil Mascaras ☐
B Dean Malenko ☐
C Eddie Guerrero ☑
D Pedro Morales ☐

14 Which team did Ric Flair and Roddy Piper defeat to win the World Tag Team Championships in 2006?

A Rated RKO ☐
B D-Generation X ☑
C The Colons ☐
D The Spirit Squad ☐

15 What WCW legend returned to WWE in 2016 and became Universal Champion at *Fastlane 2017*?

A Diamond Dallas Page ☐
B Great Muta ☐
C Sting ☐
D Goldberg ☑

woooo!!

FOR THE RECORD

16 In his lone *WrestleMania* victory, Ric Flair helped Evolution defeat which team?

.... Shield ....

Answers on pages 76-77

WrestleMania

DANIEL WITH ROWAN
VS KOFI WITH NEW DAY
WWE CHAMPIONSHIP MATCH

BACKGROUND

THE COMPETITORS

What a difference a year makes! At **WrestleMania 34**, Bryan pulled off another incredible **underdog story**, returning from serious injury to adoring chants of **"Yes!"** Now, beneath his trademark beard lies a cold scowl, and "Yes!" is what we think on the rare moments he shuts his pompous mouth! The "New" Daniel Bryan is bent on **saving the planet**, one egotistical rant at a time. Every bit the dangerous grappler he was in **friendlier times** with an added nasty streak, silencing this eco-friendly foe is a near impossible task.

DANIEL BRYAN
(WITH ROWAN)

THE BUILD-UP...

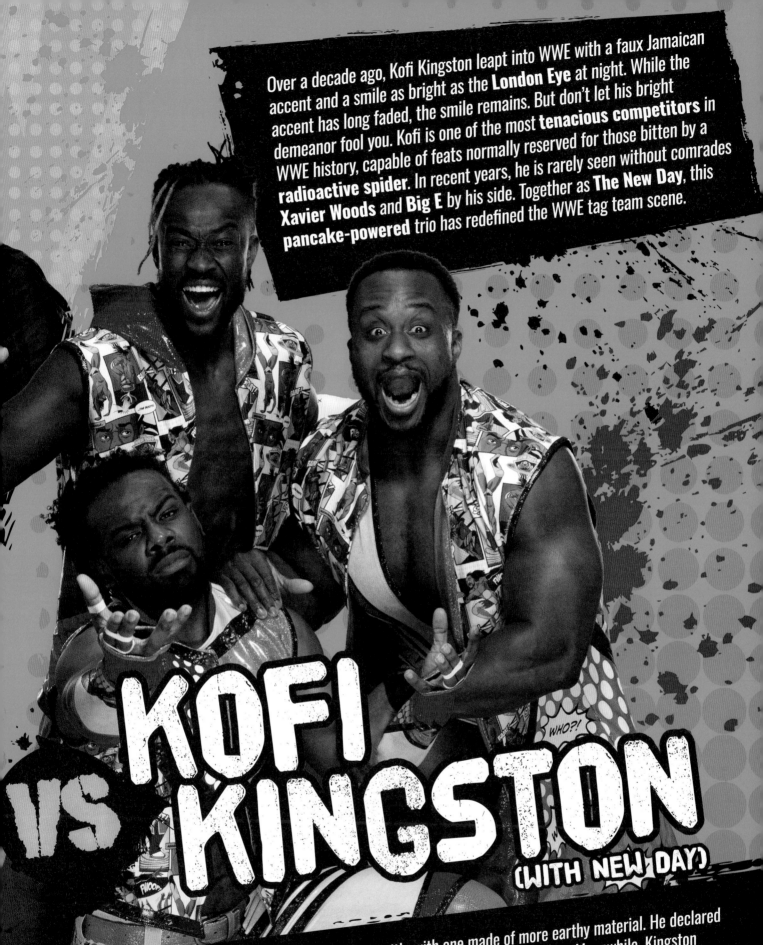

Over a decade ago, Kofi Kingston leapt into WWE with a faux Jamaican accent and a smile as bright as the **London Eye** at night. While the accent has long faded, the smile remains. But don't let his bright demeanor fool you. Kofi is one of the most **tenacious competitors** in WWE history, capable of feats normally reserved for those bitten by a radioactive spider. In recent years, he is rarely seen without comrades **Xavier Woods** and **Big E** by his side. Together as **The New Day**, this pancake-powered trio has redefined the WWE tag team scene.

KOFI
vs KINGSTON
(WITH NEW DAY)

Upon becoming WWE Champion, Daniel replaced his leather title with one made of more earthy material. He declared himself "**The Planet's Champion**" and recruited the **monstrous Rowan** to aid his cause. Meanwhile, Kingston **captured the heart** of the WWE Universe with a spirited performance at **Elimination Chamber**. Bryan scoffed at Kofi's surge in momentum. He called Kofi a "**B+ player**," the same insulting label The Authority once gave to Bryan himself. When Kofi and his New Day mates prevailed in separate Gauntlet Matches, Kofi's detractors could no longer deny his **deserved opportunity**. #KofiMania was alive in Met Life Stadium as the eleven-year veteran finally got his chance at WWE immortality.

49

WRESTLEMANIA

DANIEL (WITH ROWAN) VS KOFI (WITH NEW DAY) WWE CHAMPIONSHIP MATCH

DANIEL BRYAN VS KOFI KINGSTON
(WITH ROWAN)   (WITH NEW DAY)

THE WWE UNIVERSE CHANTS KOFI'S NAME AS HE BOUNCES DOWN THE RAMP ALONGSIDE THE NEW DAY. I'VE GOT GOOSE BUMPS!

HERE'S THE "NEW" DANIEL BRYAN, SHOWING OFF HIS "SUSTAINABLE" TITLE AS HIS HEAVY, ROWAN, CASTS A GLARE OVER AT NEW DAY.

IT'S HOLD FOR HOLD, MUSCLE AGAINST MUSCLE SO FAR...

...UNTIL A POWERFUL KICK SENDS BRYAN TUMBLING TO THE OUTSIDE...

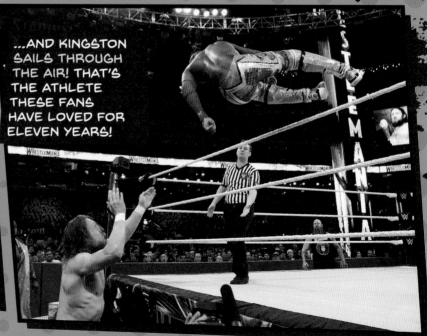

...AND KINGSTON SAILS THROUGH THE AIR! THAT'S THE ATHLETE THESE FANS HAVE LOVED FOR ELEVEN YEARS!

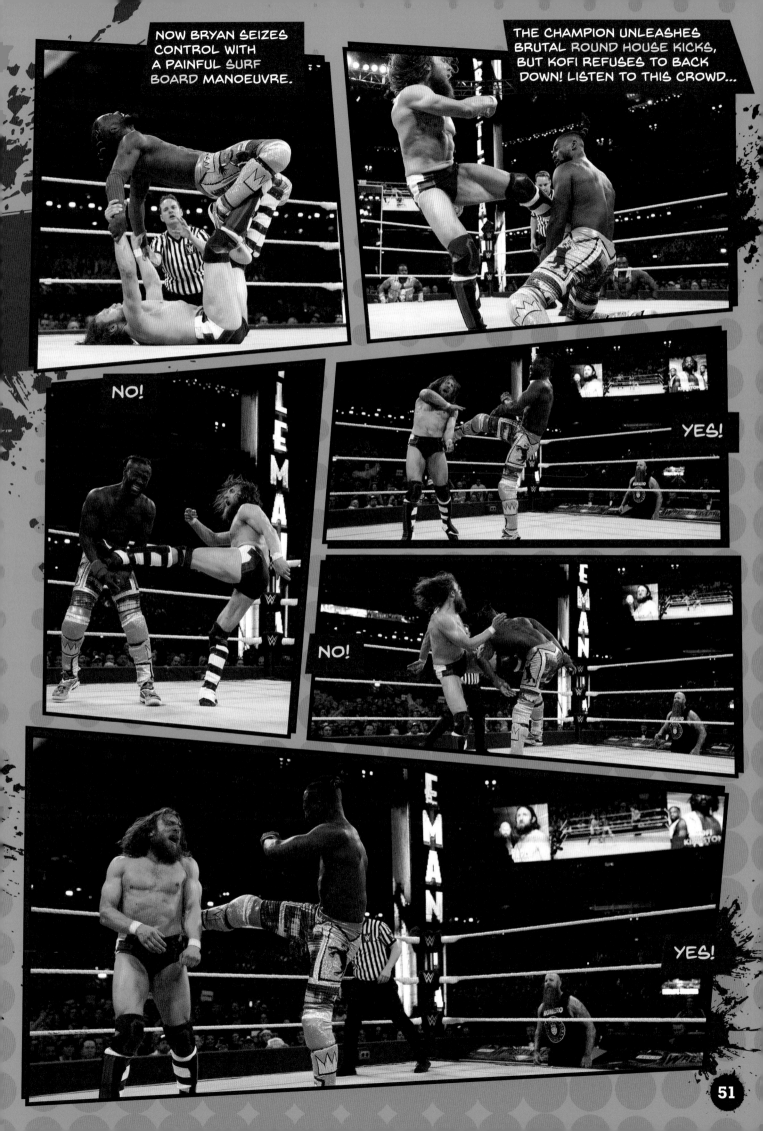

NOW BRYAN SEIZES CONTROL WITH A PAINFUL SURF BOARD MANOEUVRE.

THE CHAMPION UNLEASHES BRUTAL ROUND HOUSE KICKS, BUT KOFI REFUSES TO BACK DOWN! LISTEN TO THIS CROWD...

NO!

YES!

NO!

YES!

NEW DAY HAS TAKEN OUT ROWAN, AND KOFI TAKES ADVANTAGE WITH A JAW DROPPING AERIAL MOVE!

BACK IN THE RING, KOFI TAKES FLIGHT ONCE AGAIN...

...BUT BRYAN WAS READY FOR IT, AND NOW HE SHOWS SOME AGILITY OF HIS OWN.

DOWN ONTO KOFI LIKE A GUILLOTINE!

IS THIS WHERE THE DREAM ENDS?

BRYAN IS BACK TO WHAT HE DOES BEST, INFLICT PAIN!

A LEBELL LOCK! KINGSTON MIGHT BE OUT...NOT SO FAST. HIS HAND DIDN'T DROP.

KOFI FIGHTS OUT OF IT! IT'S HIS TURN TO DISH OUT SOME PUNISHMENT. BOOM DROP CONNECTS!

TROUBLE IN PARADISE!! GO FOR THE COVER, KOFI!!

1...2....3!! KOFI HAS DONE IT!!! HIS ELEVEN YEAR ODYSSEY HAS LED HIM TO GOLD HERE ON THE GRANDEST STAGE!!!

WOODS AND BIG E HAD THE REAL WWE TITLE WAITING FOR HIM. THEY KNEW HE COULD DO IT!

AND THE NEW WWE CHAMPION GETS A HUG FROM HIS TWO SONS. NOW THAT'S A WRESTLEMANIA MOMENT!!!

COMPETITION WINNERS

To celebrate the 20th Anniversary of SmackDown, Delzinski, Little Brother Books and WWE joined forces again to run another awesome competition. This year we asked players of the WWE 2K19 game to get creative and design a new SmackDown arena.

The winning creator received family tickets to WWE's November UK tour and their winning SmackDown arena is featured in this year's WWE Annual!

After many amazing arenas were submitted using the hashtag #LBBSD via the WWE 2K19 Community Creations for XBOX One and PS4, one epic design was chosen!

This SmackDown arena was created by
COREY WEST

And Well Done to both Keshav Jugpal and Thomas Wall, two awesome runners up!

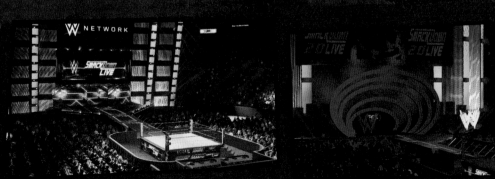

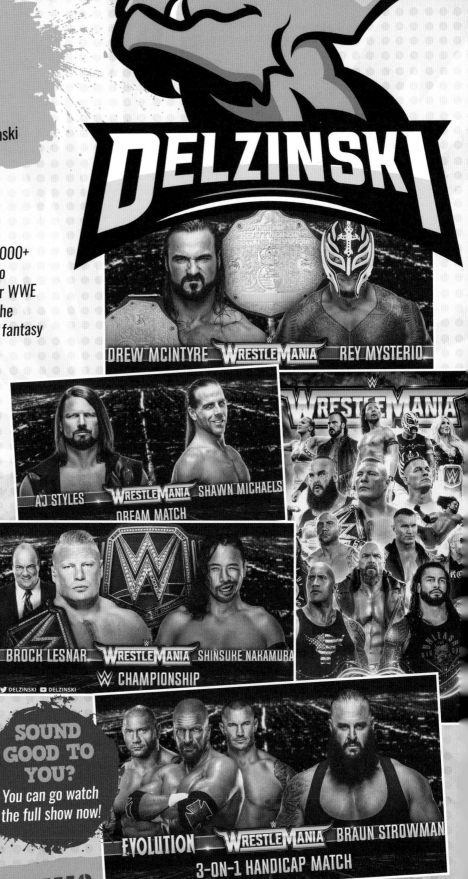

DREW MCINTYRE — WrestleMania — REY MYSTERIO

AJ STYLES — WrestleMania — SHAWN MICHAELS
DREAM MATCH

BROCK LESNAR — WrestleMania — SHINSUKE NAKAMURA
WWE CHAMPIONSHIP

DELZINSKI DELZINSKI

EVOLUTION — WrestleMania — BRAUN STROWMAN
3-ON-1 HANDICAP MATCH

DELZINSKI DELZINSKI

ABOUT ME

Delzinski's YouTube channel has 112,000+ subscribers and over 35 million video views. Why not check out his popular WWE Games Universe Mode series where he takes control of WWE, creating epic fantasy matches and enthralling storylines!

The images you see on this page are from Delzinski's WrestleMania! This particular WrestleMania fantasy event took place at the U.S Bank Stadium in Minneapolis Minnesota and showcased several dream face-offs. These included "The Phenomenal" AJ Styles vs "Mr WrestleMania" Shawn Michaels and Evolution uniting to tackle the "Monster Among Men" Braun Strowman. The "Master of the 619" Rey Mysterio faced the leader of the New World Order and World Heavyweight Champion, Drew Mcintyre and for the WrestleMania main event, Royal Rumble winner "The King of Strong Style" Shinsuke Nakamura went one-on-one with "The Beast Incarnate" and WWE Champion Brock Lesnar!

SOUND GOOD TO YOU?
You can go watch the full show now!

DID YOU KNOW?

Delzinski's favourite match of last year was at NXT UK Takeover New York where WALTER challenged the Brusierweight Pete Dunne for the United Kingdom Championship! **WHAT A MATCH!** British Strong Style at its best!

THREE'S COMPANY?

Tag team trios are all the rage these days. I like to think I started that trend when I took WWE by storm alongside my best friends in The Shield. Two guys watching your back is way better than one. Believe that! Take the below quiz and find out which team you should join as the third member!

What is your opinion on face paint?

A I liked it when I was younger
B I'd rather a beard
C It looks great...on my boot!
D Red and black, please!

What makes an ideal tag team partner?

A A sibling
B A no-nonsense tough guy
C A former rival
D An equally disturbed friend

Favorite legendary tag team?

A Too Cool & Rikishi
B The Brainbusters
C The Allied Powers
D The Road Warriors

My key to success is?

A Genetics
B My fists
C High standards
D My twisted mind

What makes you want to lose your lunch?

A Pancakes
B Flips
C Nicholas
D Pathetic humans

If you answered mostly A, you should join The Usos. You have a unique mix of grit and flair. Family always comes first because blood is thicker than water!

If you answered mostly B, you should join The Revival. You are a rough-and-tumble competitor with no time for fancy frills. All you need is a mat and an opponent and the fight is on!

If you answered mostly C, you should join The Bar. You are a pro's pro. You strive for perfection, and anyone who doesn't had better stay out of your way!

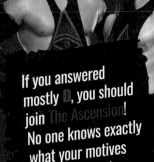

If you answered mostly D, you should join The Ascension! No one knows exactly what your motives are, only that they are not pleasant. This frightens people, and that pleases you.

TAG TEAM TURMOIL

WWE's tag team division is in great peril. It seems no one can find his partner! Draw a line to reunite each Superstar with his other half, so they can continue their quest for the Raw or *SmackDown* Tag Team Titles!

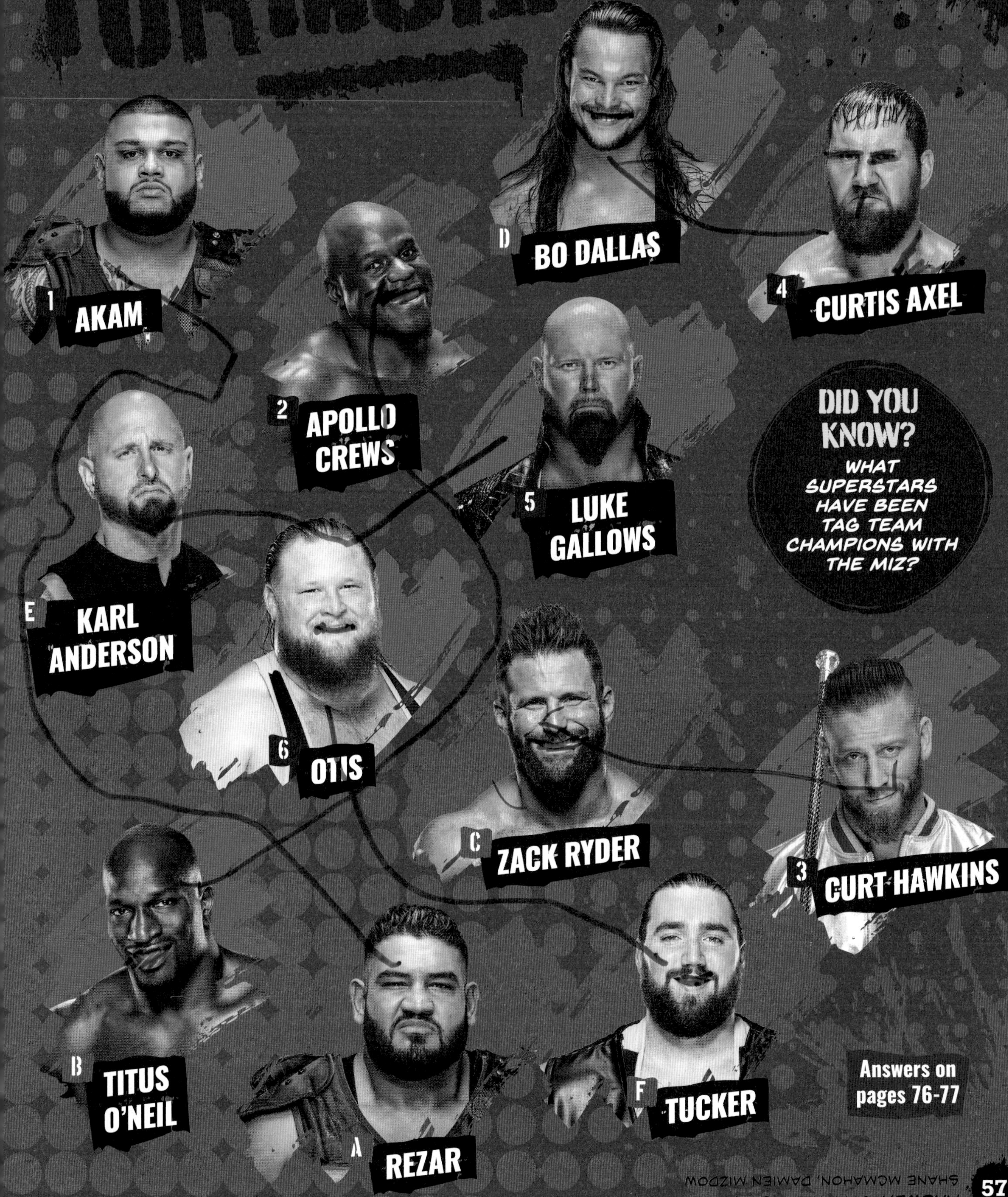

D BO DALLAS
4 CURTIS AXEL
1 AKAM
2 APOLLO CREWS
5 LUKE GALLOWS
E KARL ANDERSON
6 OTIS
C ZACK RYDER
3 CURT HAWKINS
B TITUS O'NEIL
A REZAR
F TUCKER

DID YOU KNOW?

WHAT SUPERSTARS HAVE BEEN TAG TEAM CHAMPIONS WITH THE MIZ?

Answers on pages 76-77

ANSWER: JOHN MORRISON, JOHN CENA, BIG SHOW, SHANE MCMAHON, DAMIEN MIZDOW

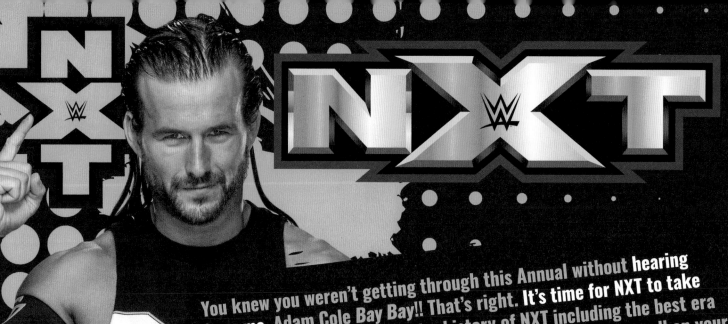

You knew you weren't getting through this Annual without hearing from me, Adam Cole Bay Bay!! That's right. It's time for NXT to take over! This quiz covers the entire history of NXT including the best era of them all, mine. Answer these brain benders and you are well on your way to joining me between the yellow ropes, and that is undisputed!

1 Who was the first-ever NXT Women's Champion
a. Paige
b. Emma
c. Sasha Banks
d. Becky Lynch

2 Who won the NXT Championship at an event in Tokyo, Japan in 2015?
a. Kevin Owens
b. Sami Zayn
c. Shinsuke Nakamura
d. Finn Bálor

3 Which multi-time Tag Team Champion used to pin opponents for 5 seconds as a singles star in NXT?
a. Harper
b. Big E
c. Xavier Woods
d. Kofi Kingston

4 Who did Kevin Owens defeat in his debut match while still NXT Champion?
a. Chris Jericho
b. Dean Ambrose
c. John Cena
d. Daniel Bryan

5 What did Tommaso Ciampa and Johnny Gargano name their NXT tag team?
a. #TBT
b. #WCW
c. #DIY
d. #LOL

6 Which of these teams never won NXT's annual Dusty Rhodes Tag Team Classic?
a. Finn Balor & Samoa Joe
b. The Revival
c. Undisputed Era
d. Authors of Pain

7 I am the first two time NXT Women's Champion.
a. Kairi Sane
b. Asuka
c. Charlotte Flair
d. Shayna Baszler

QUIZ

8 What does Undisputed Era's Adam Cole call his finishing move?
a. Last Shot
b. Last Call
c. Last Dance
d. Last Breath

9 Which NXT Superstar is from Auckland, New Zealand?
a. Rhea Ripley
b. Dakota Kai
c. Aliyah
d. Vanessa Borne

10 What is this amazing move Ricochet used to pin Adam Cole for the NXT North American Championship at NXT Takeover: Brooklyn 4.
a. 630 Splash
b. 450 Splash
c. Shooting Star Press
d. Five Start Frog Splash

11 Who is this flashy Superstar who has won the NXT North American Championship?
a. Kassius Ohno
b. Bobby Fish
c. Kona Reeves
d. Velveteen Dream

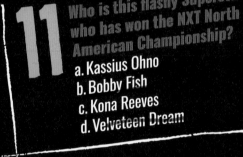

12 Which NXT UK Superstar captured the NXT UK Women's Championship at NXT UK Takeover: Blackpool?
a. Rhea Ripley
b. Toni Storm
c. Xia Brookside
d. Candy Floss

13 At what age did Tyler Bate become the first-ever NXT UK Champion?
a. 18
b. 19
c. 20
d. 21

14 What was the name of the 2019 tournament that featured Superstars from NXT, NXT UK and 205 Live?
a. War Games
b. World War 3
c. Worlds Collide
d. World of Warcraft

15 What was the name of the tag team featuring Kairi Sane and Io Shirai?
a. Sky Pirates
b. Jumping Bomb Angels
c. Boss & Hug Connection
d. Fire & Desire

Answers on pages 76-77

NXT

MEET THE GRIZZLED YOUNG VETERANS

NAMES James Drake & Zack Gibson

FROM Drake Blackpool, England
Gibson Liverpool, England

HEIGHT Drake 5' 11"
Gibson 6' 3"

WEIGHT Drake 178 lbs
Gibson 180 lbs

SIGNATURE MOVES Ticket to Mayhem
Shankly Gates

These aggressive scrappers began teaming up in 2017. Today, they can be seen roughing up the tag team division on NXT UK! Here's a look at their young WWE careers so far.

AUGUST 2018 NXT TAKEOVER BROOKLYN IV

Gibson, nicknamed "Liverpool's Number 1" **challenged Pete Dunne** for the **NXT UK Championship.** Gibson won a tournament for the right to face Dunne and **battled him throughout the summer,** falling short but proving to be a tough customer.

NOVEMBER-DECEMBER 2018 NXT UK

Drake & Gibson begin to **hit their stride** as a team, **topping Amir Jordan and Kenny Williams** in successive matches.

JANUARY 2019 NXT UK

The Grizzled Young Veterans continued to roll. **Victory over Flash Morgan Webster and Mark Andrews** earns them a spot in the NXT UK Tag Team Championship Match.

JANUARY 12 2019 NXT BLACKPOOL

Moustache Mountain gave it all they had, wearing gear inspired by the **legendary British Bulldogs.** The Young Vets would not be denied, however. They **downed Trent Seven** with a **Ticket to Mayhem** to become the inaugural NXT UK Tag Team Champions!

Drake and Gibson successfully **defended their titles** against **The Street Profits,** proving their historic reign was no fluke.

Asuka's MISSING MASK MAZE

The WWE Universe is ready for Asuka, but I'm not ready for them! My rivals plan to crimp my style by hiding my mask at the end of this maze! Help me find it so I can make an entrance befitting an Empress!

Answers on pages 76-77

WRESTLEMANIA HIGHLIGHTS

TRIPLE H DEFEATED BATISTA IN A NO HOLDS BARRED MATCH

Batista got what we wanted, and oh my, it was ugly! The Animal was so desperate to face Triple H, he **attacked 70-year old Ric Flair** to provoke him. In a decisive victory, Triple H gets the **award for coolest entrance** and most gruesome moment. He yanked Batista's nose ring out with a pair of pliers!

FINN BÁLOR DEFEATED BOBBY LASHLEY TO WIN THE INTERCONTINENTAL CHAMPIONSHIP

Becky Lynch was not the only one to do **Ireland proud**. The Demon emerged from the dark soul of Finn Bálor to **overwhelm Bobby Lashley**. Lashley and his hype man, Lio Rush, had little defence for the challenger's potent attacks. Bálor won with his signature **Coup de Grace** to Lashley's chest.

THE DOCTOR OF THUGANOMICS RETURNED

John Cena dusted off his **old rap skills** to school Elias.

62

BARON CORBIN DEFEATED KURT ANGLE IN ANGLE'S FAREWELL MATCH

Since Angle returned to WWE, Baron Corbin has been a **constant nuisance**. Angle picked Corbin as his **final opponent** looking for revenge. But Corbin was up to the task. He hit the End of Days to **turn out the lights** on the Hall of Famer's career.

AJ STYLES DEFEATED RANDY ORTON

After Orton **trash-talked** AJ's career, these two **proud Superstars** traded harsh insults for weeks. With personal pride at stake, Styles stood tall, winning with a **Phenomenal Forearm** to The Viper.

SAMOA JOE DEFEATED REY MYSTERIO TO RETAIN THE UNITED STATES CHAMPIONSHIP

Most people would be **nervous** for their **first WrestleMania** match, but most people aren't Samoa Joe. The **surly submission** master made quick work of his veteran opponent.

ZACK RYDER & CURT HAWKINS DEFEATED THE REVIVAL FOR THE RAW TAG TEAM CHAMPIONSHIP

The **native Long Islanders** came through for the home crowd. Hawkins snapped a personal **269 match losing-streak!**

THE USOS WON A FATAL 4-WAY MATCH TO RETAIN THE SMACKDOWN TAG TEAM CHAMPIONSHIPS

The Usos seized the major **WrestleMania 35** win that had **alluded them** their entire careers. With this feather in their cap, the brothers **beef up** their resume as an all-time great WWE tag team.

TONY NESE DEFEATED BUDDY MURPHY FOR THE CRUISERWEIGHT CHAMPIONSHIP

Will this be the Premier Era on 205 Live?

CARMELLA WON THE WRESTLEMANIA WOMEN'S BATTLE ROYAL

...and returned later on for a **dance break!**

BRAUN STROWMAN WON THE ANDRE THE GIANT MEMORIAL BATTLE ROYAL

The Monster Among Men finally **got his hands** on comedians Colin Jost and Michael Che!

WINNER TAKE ALL TRIPLE THREAT MATCH

WRESTLEMANIA

BACKGROUND

THE COMPETITORS

After years of playing nice while others reaped rewards, Becky became "The Man" when she let loose her unfiltered personality and her deep-seated fury in the ring. Like a modern day Stone Cold Steve Austin, this **fiery Irish terroriser** trampled her way through WWE, defying the powers that be and **rewriting the rules** on her way to the top. Despite suffering a broken face, busted ankle, multiple suspensions and even run-ins with the law, **nothing can stop "The Man"** from coming around!

BECKY LYNCH vs CHARLOTTE FLAIR

FOR THE RAW & SMACKDOWN WOMEN'S CHAMPIONSHIPS

Long considered a **beacon** of the Women's Evolution, Flair is among the most decorated Superstars in WWE. She considers herself **WWE royalty**, and it is hard to argue. Her regal attire, cocky swagger and championship resume evoke memories of her **legendary dad**, Ric Flair. With shocking athletic ability that surpasses even her proud pop, winning is simply second nature to Charlotte. Like it or hate it, learn to love it, because Charlotte Flair might just be **the best thing going**. Wooooo!

RONDA ROUSEY

The **Baddest Woman on the Planet** spent a lifetime **beating people up** in Mixed Martial Arts and other combat sports, becoming a household name worldwide. With little left to prove, Rousey pursued her **childhood dream** - WWE. Like her hero "Rowdy" Roddy Piper, she broke into WWE with fearless grit and a brash attitude. Within her first year, she became **Raw Women's Champion** and sent a gauntlet of tough challengers sulking to the locker room looking for an ice pack!

VS

After a **gutsy win** in the Women's Royal Rumble Match, Becky Lynch **wasted no time** challenging the **Raw Women's Champion**, Rousey, to a **WrestleMania showdown**. But Becky's fighting spirit backfired when she crossed the McMahon family, who gave Charlotte her spot in the match. "The Man" would **earn her way back**, while Charlotte **raised the stakes** by becoming **SmackDown** Women's Champion. This set the stage for a historic Winner Take All Triple Threat Match. The first three women to headline **WrestleMania** would do so with both women's titles on the line!

WINNER TAKE ALL TRIPLE THREAT MATCH

BECKY LYNCH VS CHARLOTTE FLAIR VS RONDA ROUSEY

HISTORY WILL BE MADE TONIGHT! IT'S THE FIRST WOMEN'S MAIN EVENT IN WRESTLEMANIA HISTORY, AND HERE COMES THE BADDEST WOMEN ON THE PLANET!

CHARLOTTE ENTERS THE BUILDING JUST LIKE HER DAD, STYLIN' AND PROFILIN'!

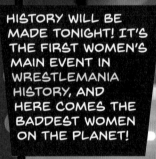

THE MAN HAS ARRIVED. IS THERE ANY DOUBT WHO THE FAN FAVORITE IS TONIGHT?

SO MUCH BAD BLOOD BETWEEN THESE THREE SUPERSTARS...

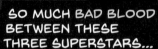

THEY JUST TAKE TURNS...

POUNDING ON EACH OTHER!

FOR THE RAW & SMACKDOWN WOMEN'S CHAMPIONSHIPS

HERE COMES BECKY WITH A BASEBALL SLIDE SENDING RONDA TO THE FLOOR!

IF THE CHALLENGER WANTS TO FIGHT OUTSIDE THE RING, THAT'S FINE WITH ROUSEY.

CHARLOTTE LOOKS TO WEAKEN RONDA...

BUT FLAIR SWOOPS IN AND HURLS HER INTO THE BARRIER!

...WITH SOME CLASSIC FLAIR MOVES! WOOOOO!

RONDA HANGS TOUGH, AND HERE COMES THE MAN FROM OUT OF NOWHERE!

UH OH...

ALL THREE SUPERSTARS BATTLING TO THE BITTER END.

THERE GOES CHARLOTTE THROUGH A TABLE!

AND NOW RONDA HAS BECKY IN THE PIPER'S PIT! IT'S ALL OVER, BUT WAIT...

A REVERSAL INTO A CRUCIFIX PIN! 1...2...3!! BECKY HAS DONE IT!

THE MAN WALKED IN EMPTYHANDED, AND LEAVES WITH TWO TITLES! WHAT A WRESTLEMANIA!

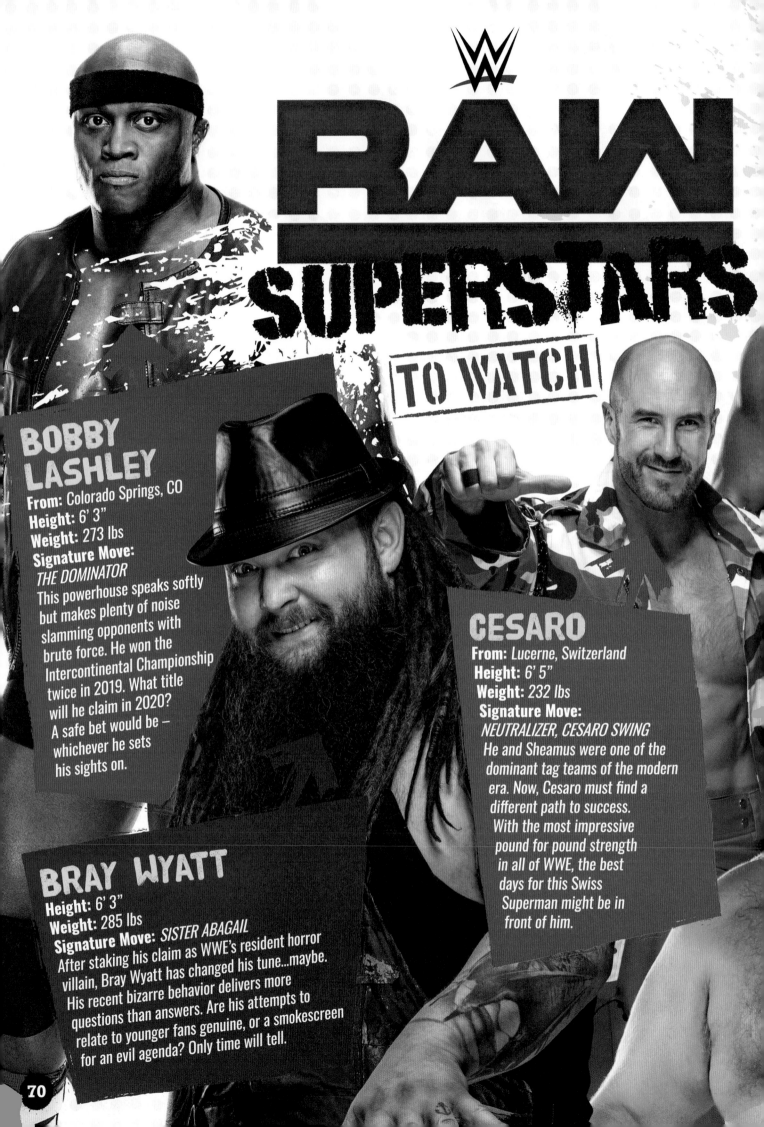

RAW SUPERSTARS TO WATCH

BOBBY LASHLEY

From: Colorado Springs, CO
Height: 6' 3"
Weight: 273 lbs
Signature Move:
THE DOMINATOR
This powerhouse speaks softly but makes plenty of noise slamming opponents with brute force. He won the Intercontinental Championship twice in 2019. What title will he claim in 2020? A safe bet would be — whichever he sets his sights on.

BRAY WYATT

Height: 6' 3"
Weight: 285 lbs
Signature Move: *SISTER ABAGAIL*
After staking his claim as WWE's resident horror villain, Bray Wyatt has changed his tune...maybe. His recent bizarre behavior delivers more questions than answers. Are his attempts to relate to younger fans genuine, or a smokescreen for an evil agenda? Only time will tell.

CESARO

From: Lucerne, Switzerland
Height: 6' 5"
Weight: 232 lbs
Signature Move:
NEUTRALIZER, CESARO SWING
He and Sheamus were one of the dominant tag teams of the modern era. Now, Cesaro must find a different path to success. With the most impressive pound for pound strength in all of WWE, the best days for this Swiss Superman might be in front of him.

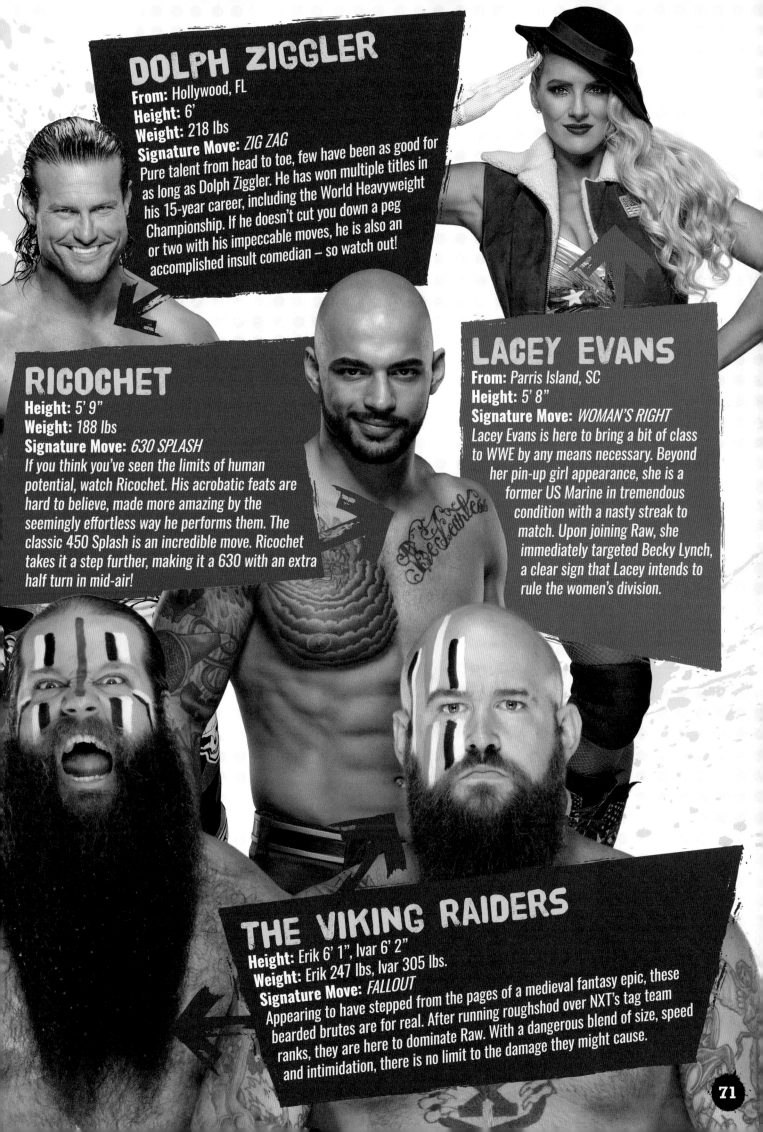

DOLPH ZIGGLER

From: Hollywood, FL
Height: 6'
Weight: 218 lbs
Signature Move: *ZIG ZAG*

Pure talent from head to toe, few have been as good for as long as Dolph Ziggler. He has won multiple titles in his 15-year career, including the World Heavyweight Championship. If he doesn't cut you down a peg or two with his impeccable moves, he is also an accomplished insult comedian – so watch out!

RICOCHET

Height: 5' 9"
Weight: 188 lbs
Signature Move: *630 SPLASH*

If you think you've seen the limits of human potential, watch Ricochet. His acrobatic feats are hard to believe, made more amazing by the seemingly effortless way he performs them. The classic 450 Splash is an incredible move. Ricochet takes it a step further, making it a 630 with an extra half turn in mid-air!

LACEY EVANS

From: Parris Island, SC
Height: 5' 8"
Signature Move: *WOMAN'S RIGHT*

Lacey Evans is here to bring a bit of class to WWE by any means necessary. Beyond her pin-up girl appearance, she is a former US Marine in tremendous condition with a nasty streak to match. Upon joining Raw, she immediately targeted Becky Lynch, a clear sign that Lacey intends to rule the women's division.

THE VIKING RAIDERS

Height: Erik 6' 1", Ivar 6' 2"
Weight: Erik 247 lbs, Ivar 305 lbs.
Signature Move: *FALLOUT*

Appearing to have stepped from the pages of a medieval fantasy epic, these bearded brutes are for real. After running roughshod over NXT's tag team ranks, they are here to dominate Raw. With a dangerous blend of size, speed and intimidation, there is no limit to the damage they might cause.

WELCOME WWE TO THE

HALL OF FAME

2019

D-GENERATION X

Members: Triple H, Shawn Michaels, X-Pac, Billy Gunn, Road Dogg & Chyna

Claim to Fame: Kickstarting the rebellious Attitude Era in WWE, offending the censors, driving Mr. McMahon crazy!

"YOU MAKE THE RULES, AND WE'LL BREAK 'EM!!"

"WHAT WE HAVE HERE ARE TWO HARTS BEATING AS ONE!"

THE HART FOUNDATION

Members: Bret Hart & Jim "The Anvil" Neidhart

Claim to Fame: Making tag teams the main event, members of WWE's revered Hart family, two-time World Tag Team Champions .

THE HONKY TONK MAN

Claim to Fame: Longest reigning Intercontinental Champion of all time, wielding a guitar long before Elias, antagonizing WWE's greatest heroes of the 80s.

"I'M COOL, I'M COCKY AND I'M BAD!"

THE NINTH WONDER OF THE WORLD

This DX enforcer received a long-awaited induction. Chyna was so powerful, she matched strengths with male stars like Chris Jericho and Jeff Jarrett in one-on-one matches. She is the only women to ever win the Intercontinental Championship!

DID YOU KNOW?

WHICH INTERCONTINENTAL CHAMPION INVENTED THE "HONK-O-METER"?

TORRIE WILSON

Claim to Fame: Turning heads, stopping traffic, and kicking butt while doing it!

"I AM THE EPITOME OF THE ALL-AMERICAN GOOD GIRL."

DID YOU KNOW?

WHO WAS THE FIRST SUPERSTAR TO BE INDUCTED INTO THE WWE HALL OF FAME TWICE?

HARLEM HEAT

Members: Booker T & Stevie Ray
Claim to Fame: Most Tag Team Championships in WCW history (10), one of the most dominant 1990s tag teams in all of sports entertainment.

"YOU EITHER ROLL WITH US, OR WE'RE GONNA ROLL RIGHT OVER YOU!"

WELCOME BACK STACY KEIBLER

The stunning Superstar-turned-actress returned to induct her friend, Torrie, into the Hall of Fame.

BRUTUS THE BARBER BEEFCAKE

Claim to Fame: Trimming the hair off his foes with giant sheers, forming the Mega Maniacs with Hulk Hogan, hosting The Barber Shop talk show.

"CUTTIN' AND STRUTTIN'!"

ANSWER: SANTINO MARELLA. SANTINO ASPIRED TO BEAT HONKY TONK'S 454 DAY INTERCONTINENTAL CHAMPIONSHIP REIGN. THE GOOFY INVENTION COUNTED HOW MANY DAYS HE HAD LEFT.

ANSWER: RIC FLAIR, AS HIMSELF AND WITH THE FOUR HORSEMEN

73

REMEMBERING MEAN GENE

"MEAN" GENE OKERLUND
DECEMBER 19 1942 – JANUARY 2 2019

With his even-keeled grace and sharp wit, famed announcer "Mean" Gene Okerlund was the unmistakable voice of WWE for a generation. The WWE Universe fondly remembers his most amusing moments. Okerlund was nicknamed "Mean" Gene as a tribute to his mild-mannered style. Hulk Hogan, Ric Flair, "Macho Man" Randy Savage and more gave their best interviews with "Mean" Gene asking the questions.

"Mean" Gene hosted talk shows like Tuesday Night Titans, where he got to the bottom of WWE's hottest stories. His vocal talents were not just for speaking. "Mean" Gene sung at the first WrestleMania and performed the song "Tutti Frutti" on WWE's The Wrestling Album.

He was not afraid to shed his tux and get serious! "Gene-o-Mania" ran wild when he teamed with The Hulkster! For "Mean" Gene, getting up close and personal with WWE's most outlandish Superstars (and their pets), was just part of the job.

While retired, he made surprise appearances in WWE. He and fellow funnyman Bobby "The Brain" Heenan called the action in the WrestleMania X-7 Gimmick Battle Royal.

In 2006, old friend Hogan inducted him into the WWE Hall of Fame. He was the first-ever announcer inducted, a deserved honour!

LET ME TELL YOU SOMETHING.
"MEAN" GENE! YOU'LL BE MISSED.

WRESTLEMANIA

What's Next?

A lot can happen in a year, especially in WWE. By the time you pick up your 2021 Annual, you can bet there will be new champions, new Superstars and plenty of teams formed (and broken). Use the space below to jot down your predictions. After WrestleMania 36 on April 5 in Tampa Bay, Florida, check back to see if you were right!

THE MAIN EVENT OF WRESTLEMANIA 36 WILL BE _brock vs Drew_

no body WILL TURN ON HIS/HER TAG TEAM PARTNER(S),

cronk manie WILL BE THE HOST OF WRESTLEMANIA 36.

AFTER A LONG TIME AWAY, _edge_ WILL MAKE A SURPRISE RETURN TO WWE.

VILLAINOUS SUPERSTAR _~~seth~~ rollins IDK_ WILL CHANGE HIS/HER ATTITUDE AND BE CHEERED BY THE WWE UNIVERSE.

NXT SUPERSTAR _rhea ridley_ WILL MAKE THE BIGGEST IMPACT ON RAW OR SMACKDOWN.

THE MATCH OF THE YEAR WILL BE _edge ~~orton~~_ VS. _orton_ AT _wrestlemanie, Backlas_

otis WILL CLAIM THE MONEY IN THE BANK BRIEFCASE.

A NEW SUPERSTAR WILL DEBUT! FILL IN HIS/HER STATS AND BIO BELOW:

NAME _matti riddle_

FROM _Allentown, Pe_

HEIGHT _6'2_

WEIGHT _216lb 98kg_

SIGNATURE MOVES _fros splash, knee strik_

BIO _arm bar_

ANSWERS

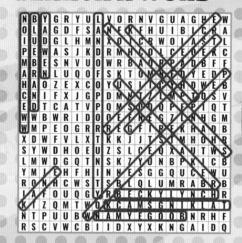

44
ALEXA-GRAMS
1: TWISTED
2: COLUMBUS
3: GODDESS
4: FURY
5: MOMENT OF BLISS
6: COFFEE
7: SUPERSTAR
8: CHAMPION
9: EVOLUTION
10: FIVE FEET

45
205 LIVE CRUISERWEIGHT CROSSWORD

46-47
LEGENDS QUIZ
1: d
2: b
3: c
4: a
5: b
6: a
7: d
8: b
9: a
10: d
11: c
12: a
13: c
14: d
15: d
16: The Rock n' Sock Connection

57
TAG TEAM TURMOIL
1: Akam – **A:** Rezar
2: Apollo Crews – **B:** Titus O'Neil
3: Curt Hawkins – **C:** Zack Ryder
4: Curtis Axel – **D:** Bo Dallas
5: Luke Gallows – **E:** Karl Anderson
6: Otis – **F:** Tucker

58-59
NXT QUIZ
1: a
2: d
3: b
4: c
5: c
6: b
7: d
8: a
9: b
10: a
11: d
12: b
13: b
14: b
15: a

61
ASUKA'S MISSING MASK MAZE